Skills Coach
Social Studies
Intermediate

Coach™
America's Best for Student Success®

D1609352

Triumph Learning®

A Haights Cross Communications ® Company

Acknowledgments

The author would like to thank the following:

The Museum of the City of New York for kind permission to use materials in their possession—photographs of life in the New York City area, circa 1900

The Library of Virginia for permission to use a reproduction of the painting by Jack Clifton entitled "First Legislature in the New World"

Gisele Laliberte and the World Health Organization for permission to reprint maps on the incidence of malaria in Africa

John LeFeber and the National Council on Economic Education for permission to use data on U.S. exports and imports

The Senate House Museum, Kingston, New York, for permission to quote from the "Account Book of Peter Van Gassbeek"

The author has also made use of materials in the following collections:

Library of Congress, Prints and Photographs Division
National Oceanic and Atmospheric Administration Collections
Franklin D. Roosevelt Digital Archives
National Park Service Collections
Royal Photographic Society (of London)

The author has also drawn on material in the following sources:

John Adams by David McCullough, for two letters by John Adams

The Hungry Years, a Narrative History of the Great Depression, by T.H. Watkins, for accounts of the Great Depression

Theodore Rex by Edmund Morris, for a letter from Captain Butt about President Theodore Roosevelt

Life in Colonial America by Elizabeth George Speare, for extracts from Gov. Winthrop's Journal, and the Stratford Town Records

Empire Express by David Haward Bain, for an extract from a letter to Oliver Ames of the Union Pacific Railroad

Encyclopedia of Black America

Extracts from letters published in *Woodstock Times* in 2003

The White House for George W. Bush's 2002 State of the Union Address

Skills Coach, Social Studies, Intermediate
75NA
ISBN-10: 1-58620-610-9
ISBN-13: 978-1-58620-610-9

Author: Vivienne Hodges, Ph.D.
Cover Image: Terry Why/Index Stock Imagery

Triumph Learning® 136 Madison Avenue, 7th Floor, New York, NY 10016
Kevin McAliley, President and Chief Executive Officer

Table of Contents

Introduction

A good social studies student must master skills as well as content. Content includes information about history, geography, civics, and economics. Analysis, interpretation, identification, generalization—these are the skills that help you to understand social studies content. This book will help you to master these skills. It will not teach you facts about history, civics, and the other social sciences. But it will help you to interpret the maps, graphics, time lines, documents, and pictures that illustrate these facts.

Social studies skills are important when you read your textbooks. Texts are filled with quotes and with graphs, pictures, and maps that illustrate a topic. These graphics make it easier to understand a topic. It is easier to understand a time line of events than a list of dates. It is easier to understand how a government budgets its money from a pie chart than from a paragraph of written text.

Social studies skills are also important when you take tests. In some tests, each question asks you to interpret the documents and graphics you are shown. You don't need any prior knowledge! Sometimes you need to combine the information in graphics and documents with what you already know to answer a question. In both cases, you must be able to make sense of the graphics.

In addition to social studies skills, this book will teach you test-taking strategies that can help you to increase the number of questions you answer correctly. One important test-taking strategy is to get the most use you can out of the information you are given. For example, some tests show you photos, graphs, and original documents on a single topic and then ask you to write an essay on the topic. The section on test-taking will teach you how to make these graphics and documents work for you.

Because tests are written, this book begins with a section on reading and writing skills. These skills include being able to draw conclusions from what you read and to identify the main idea of a passage. While many test questions are multiple-choice, others ask you to write out your answer. This may be just a word or a sentence, or it may be a whole essay. Many students find that writing is a real challenge. Help is at hand! This book teaches you how to construct an essay and how to edit what you have written.

Most every page in this book teaches you a skill and then asks you questions about it. If the text includes a word that may be new to you, its meaning will be spelled out in a glossary right there on the page. Chapters are combined into sections—map-reading, test-taking, and so on. Each section ends with a skills review.

The book begins with a test. Your answers will tell your teacher which skills you have already mastered and which you need to work on. The book also ends with a practice test. Both tests have the same difficulty level. But we're sure you will find the second test much easier than the first!

Diagnostic Pre-test

Plantation owner with sharecroppers in the Mississippi Delta, 1936

1 According to its caption, this photograph includes a group of *sharecroppers*. What kind of work do *sharecroppers* do?

A Building

B Farming

C Food preparation

D Manufacturing

2 What inference can you make about relations between the plantation owner and the sharecroppers?

F The owner was a good man to work for.

G The owner was a powerful figure, and the sharecroppers were economically dependent on him.

H The owner was borrowing money from the sharecroppers to make ends meet.

J There was no economic or social difference between them.

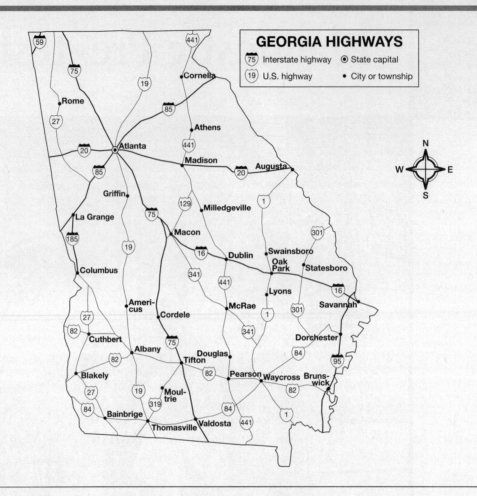

GEORGIA HIGHWAYS

75 Interstate highway ⦿ State capital
19 U.S. highway • City or township

3 What is Georgia's state capital?

A Athens

B Atlanta

C Augusta

D Savannah

4 Which of the following is an interstate highway?

F Route 1

G Route 19

H Route 75

J Route 301

5 Which highway connects Bainbridge in the southwest of the state with Dorchester in the east?

A Route 19

B Route 27

C Route 84

D Route 319

6 Describe the <u>most</u> direct route between Rome in the northwest and Milledgeville in the center of the state.

_____

_____

_____

_____

Hartford, March 28, 1885

Frank A. Nichols, Esq.,
Secretary, Concord Free Trade Club.

Dear Sir, — I am in receipt of your favor of the 24th instant, conveying the gratifying intelligence that I have been made an honorary member of the Free Trade Club of Concord, Massachusetts, and I desire to express to the club, through you, my grateful sense of the high compliment thus paid me....

A committee of the public library of your town have condemned and excommunicated my last book [*Huckleberry Finn*] and doubled its sale. This generous action of theirs must necessarily benefit me in one or two additional ways. For instance, it will deter other libraries from buying the book; and you are doubtless aware that one book in a public library prevents the sale of a sure ten and a possible hundred of its mates. And, secondly, it will cause the purchasers of the book to read it, out of curiosity, instead of merely intending to do so, after the usual way of the world and library committees; and then they will discover, to my great advantage and their own indignant disappointment, that there is nothing objectionable in the book after all...

Thanking you again, dear sir, and gentlemen,

I remain,

Your obliged servant,
S. L. Clemens
[Mark Twain]

7 **What does Mark Twain mean when he says that the Concord Public Library has *excommunicated* his latest book?**

A   Library officials have banned it from their shelves.

B   Library officials have complained about the book to the Catholic Church.

C   The library has bought many copies of it.

D   The library has asked for a discount on the price of the book.

8 **Why does Twain say he is pleased if libraries choose not to buy his book?**

F   Because he hopes the library will buy a complete set of his works rather than a single book

G   Because it will force people who want to read his book to buy it

H   Because it will keep indecent books away from the general public

J   Because it will mean the libraries can buy more children's books

9 **Reading between the lines, how would you guess Twain really feels about the action of the Concord Public Library?**

A   Disgusted

B   Pleased

C   Surprised

D   Worried

10 **Someone who believes in free speech might see the library's decision as an act of —**

F   acceptance

G   censorship

H   cruelty

J   intelligence

Major Events Leading to the Civil War

1820	1850	1852	1854	1856	1858	1860

1820
Missouri Compromise: Maine to be a free state and Missouri a slave state: slavery banned north of latitude 36°30'

1850
Compromise: California a free state, New Mexico & Utah opened to slavery; harsh fugitive slave law; slave trade abolished in Washington, D.C.

1852
Uncle Tom's Cabin published; many readers learn to hate slavery

1854
Anti-slavery Northerners form Republican Party

1854
Kansas-Nebraska Act: slavery now legal north of latitude 36°30'

1857
Dred Scott Case

1859
John Brown raids U.S. arms depot

1860
Lincoln elected President

1860–61
Southern states leave Union

---

11 What is the meaning of the diagonal white slash in the time line?

_____

_____

_____

_____

12 How many years after the first compromise over slavery did Southern states begin to leave the Union?

F 30 years

G 40 years

H 50 years

J 60 years

13 How did the Kansas-Nebraska Act reverse the Missouri Compromise?

A It made slavery legal north of latitude 36°30'.

B It outlawed slavery north of latitude 36°30'.

C It said that Congress had no power over the states.

D It said that slavery was now legal in Maine but not in Missouri.

14 Which event was the "last straw" so far as the Southern states were concerned?

F John Brown's raid

G The Dred Scott decision

H The election of Abraham Lincoln as President

J The publication of *Uncle Tom's Cabin*

15 Which of the following events might also be included on this time line?

A The adoption of the Thirteenth Amendment abolishing slavery in 1865

B The Lincoln-Douglas debates of 1858, which intensified pro- and anti-slavery opinions

C The Oregon Compromise of 1846, which settled the boundary in the northwest between the U.S. and Canada

D The Peace of Paris of 1783, which ended the Revolutionary War

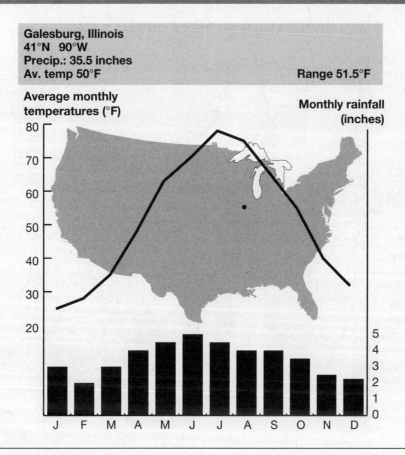

Galesburg, Illinois
41°N   90°W
Precip.: 35.5 inches
Av. temp 50°F   **Range 51.5°F**

Average monthly
temperatures (°F)   **Monthly rainfall**
                                          (inches)

---

16 **Which is the hottest month in Galesburg?**

  F June

  G July

  H August

  J September

17 **What is the average year-round temperature in Galesburg?**

  A 35°F

  B 50°F

  C 51.5°F

  D 80°F

18 **Which is the driest month in Galesburg?**

  F February

  G March

  H November

  J December

19 **How many inches of rain typically fall each August in Galesburg?**

  A One inch

  B Two inches

  C Three inches

  D Four inches

POPULATION AT RISK FOR MALARIA

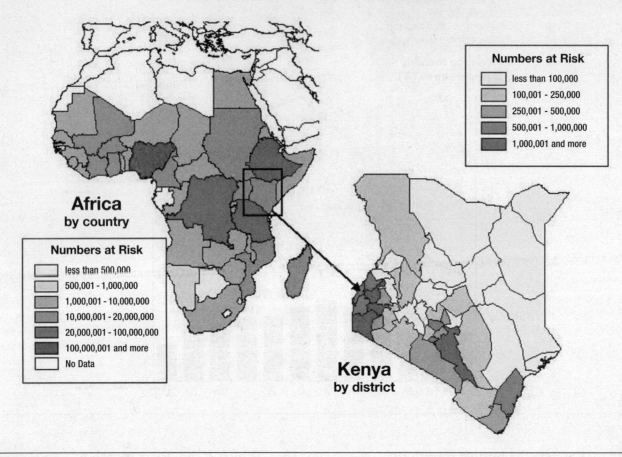

Numbers at Risk
- less than 100,000
- 100,001 - 250,000
- 250,001 - 500,000
- 500,001 - 1,000,000
- 1,000,001 and more

Africa
by country

Numbers at Risk
- less than 500,000
- 500,001 - 1,000,000
- 1,000,001 - 10,000,000
- 10,000,001 - 20,000,000
- 20,000,001 - 100,000,000
- 100,000,001 and more
- No Data

Kenya
by district

---

20 The maps above tell you —

  F how many people in different parts of Africa might contract malaria

  G the names of the African nations that are most affected by AIDS

  H the population of the nations of Africa

  J why there is more malaria in Kenya than in other parts of Africa

21 In which part of Africa is there the <u>least</u> information about malaria?

  A East Africa

  B North Africa

  C South Africa

  D West Africa

22 How many people are at risk of contracting malaria in most of the districts of Kenya?

  F Less than half a million

  G Between one million and ten million

  H Over 100 million

  J There is no data available

23 In which part of Kenya do citizens have the <u>greatest</u> risk of catching malaria?

  A The east

  B The north

  C The northeast

  D The southwest

"Is that the best care you could take of my cat?" 1912 Engraving by H.M. Wilder

24 Theodore Roosevelt was President until 1908. In the election of that year, he supported the candidacy of his fellow Republican, William Howard Taft. By 1912 when this cartoon was made, Taft had been President for four years. What does the cat in this cartoon represent?

_____

_____

25 Why would you guess Roosevelt is scowling and Taft is smiling?

_____

_____

_____

_____

_____

_____

OPENING REMARKS FROM PRESIDENT GEORGE W. BUSH'S STATE OF THE UNION ADDRESS, JANUARY 2002

Mr. Speaker, Vice President Cheney, Members of Congress, distinguished guests, and fellow citizens:

As we gather tonight, our nation is at war, our economy is in recession, and the civilized world faces unprecedented dangers. Yet the state of our Union has never been stronger.

We last met in an hour of shock and suffering. In four short months, our nation has comforted the victims; begun to rebuild New York and the Pentagon; rallied a great coalition; captured, arrested, and rid the world of thousands of terrorists; destroyed Afghanistan's terrorist training camps; saved a people from starvation; and freed a country from brutal oppression.

The American flag flies again over our embassy in Kabul. Terrorists who once occupied Afghanistan now occupy cells at Guantanamo Bay [in Cuba]. And terrorist leaders who urged followers to sacrifice their lives are running for their own.

America and Afghanistan are now allies against terror... we will be partners in rebuilding that country... and this evening we welcome the distinguished interim leader of a liberated Afghanistan: Chairman Hamid Karzai.

The last time we met in this chamber, the mothers and daughters of Afghanistan were captives in their own homes, forbidden from working or going to school. Today women are free, and are part of Afghanistan's new government, and we welcome the new Minister of Women's Affairs, Doctor Sima Samar.

---

26 The opening sentence refers to a war. Where was this war fought?

F Afghanistan   **H** Iraq

G Cuba   **J** Kuwait

27 You can infer that the capital of the nation where this war was fought is —

A Baghdad

B Guantanamo Bay

C Kabul

D Washington, D.C.

28 To which events does the President refer in the paragraph that begins "We last met..."?

F The bombing of U.S. embassies

G The capture of Osama Bin Laden

H The destruction of the Iraqi oil fields

J The 2001 terrorist attacks on New York and Washington, D.C.

29 What is the central purpose of this extract from President Bush's speech?

A To describe the horrors of life under a terrorist regime

B To emphasize that the United States is winning the war against terrorism

C To encourage Americans to send their money to help rebuild Afghanistan

D To explain the strategy that U.S. forces are using against the enemy

30 President Bush talks of the *unprecedented* dangers faced by the civilized world. What does *unprecedented* mean?

F Mysterious

G Never experienced before

H Surprising

J Tremendous

Nebraska City, Nebraska, about 1908

31 Besides the caption, what <u>most</u> helps you to date this photograph?

A The buildings

B The trees

C The vehicles

D The weather

32 Kingston, New York, is the capital or county seat of Ulster County. This is where the county courthouse is located. The building in the bottom left of the photograph is the Otoe County Courthouse. What does this tell you about Nebraska City?

F It is located in Ulster County.

G It used to be called Kingston.

H It is in New York State.

J It is the county capital.

33 How would you guess the main street of Nebraska City differed from the main streets of cities like New York and Chicago in 1908?

A Nebraska City had no shops on its sidewalks.

B Nebraska City had very few vehicles.

C The main streets of New York and Chicago were much wider, flatter, and straighter.

D The main streets of New York and Chicago had far fewer street signs.

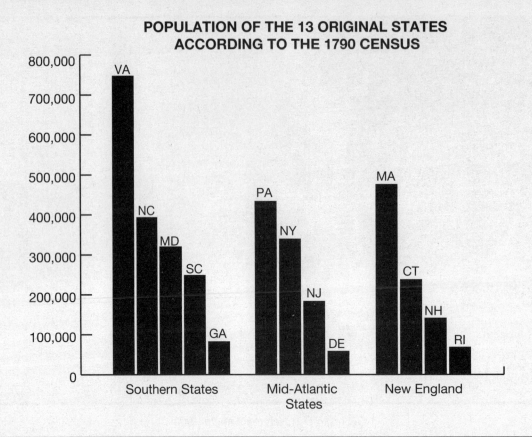

POPULATION OF THE 13 ORIGINAL STATES ACCORDING TO THE 1790 CENSUS

34 Which of the following is a Mid-Atlantic state?

F   Connecticut (CT)

G   Delaware (DE)

H   Massachusetts (MA)

J   Virginia (VA)

35 Which two states had the largest populations in 1790?

A   Massachusetts (MA) and Pennsylvania (PA)

B   New York (NY) and Pennsylvania (PA)

C   Virginia (VA) and Massachusetts (MA)

D   Virginia (VA) and Pennsylvania (PA)

36 The population of which state was closest to 300,000 in 1790?

F   Connecticut (CT)

G   Maryland (MD)

H   New York (NY)

J   South Carolina (SC)

37 About how many people lived in New England when this census was taken?

A   Half a million

B   Three-quarters of a million

C   One million

D   Two million

FEDERAL GOVERNMENT SPENDING

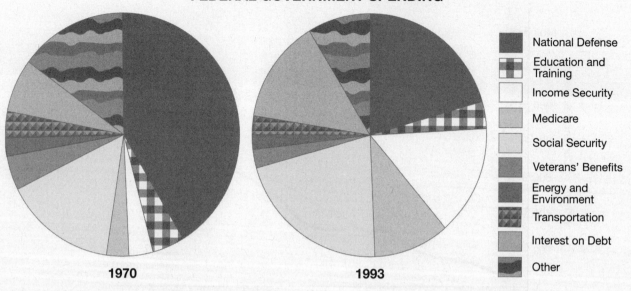

National Defense

Education and Training

Income Security

Medicare

Social Security

Veterans' Benefits

Energy and Environment

Transportation

Interest on Debt

Other

1970

1993

38 On what item did the federal government spend nearly half its budget in 1970, but less than a quarter of its budget in 1993?

F   Education and Training

G   Interest on Debt

H   Miscellaneous Expenses

J   National Defense

39 In 1993 the federal government spent a larger proportion of its budget than it did in 1970 on all of the following *except* —

A   Interest on Debt

B   Medicare

C   Social Security

D   Transportation

40 What was the biggest budget item in 1993?

F   Income Security

G   Medicare

H   National Defense

J   Social Security

41 Create a pie chart for an imaginary nation. The table below tells you what percentage of the annual budget this nation spent on different items. Label each slice of the pie. (No need to use shading.)

National Defense	30%
Human Services	25%
Interest on Debt	15%
Education and Training	10%
Energy and Environment	10%
Transportation	5%
Other	5%

GOVERNMENT EXPENSES

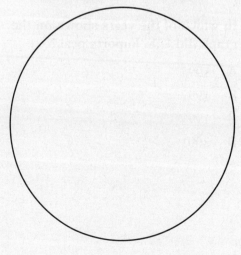

EXPORTS AND IMPORTS OF GOODS AND SERVICES

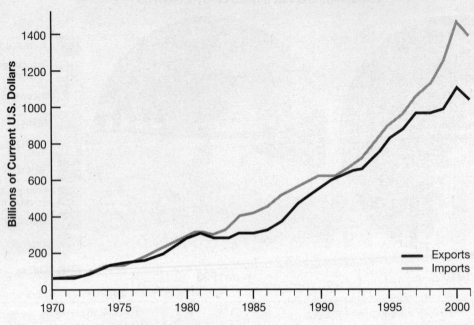

42 What general statement can you make about imports and exports between 1970 and 2000?

F Both exports and imports increased dramatically until about 1999.

G Both imports and exports declined during the 1970s.

H Exports increased and imports decreased.

J Imports increased and exports decreased.

43 In which of the years shown on the graph did U.S. imports peak?

A 1995

B 1997

C 1999

D 2001

44 What was the value of U.S. imports in 1990, measured in today's dollars?

F About 500 billion dollars

G About 600 billion dollars

H About 700 billion dollars

J About 800 billion dollars

45 A trade deficit occurs when a nation's imports exceed its exports. About when did the U.S. trade deficit begin?

A 1970

B 1973

C 1976

D 1991

46 Which of the following years saw the smallest trade deficit??

F 1991

G 1995

H 1999

J 2001

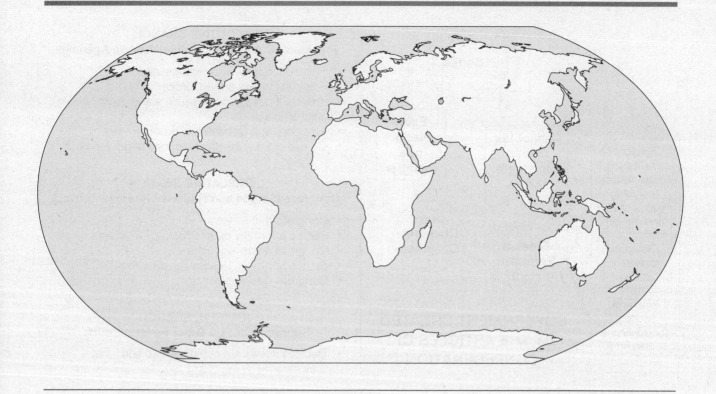

47 Label the four oceans on this map of the world.

48 Label the seven continents on this map of the world.

49 Draw a rough outline of each of the countries listed below on this map of the world, and label each one:

- Brazil
- Canada
- India
- Saudi Arabia
- Spain
- United States

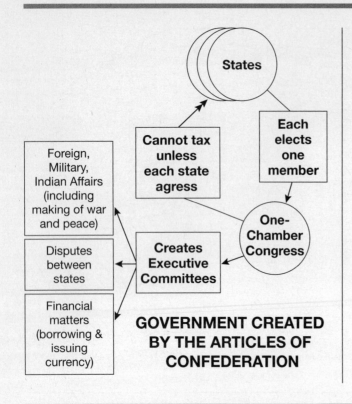

States

Cannot tax unless each state agress

Each elects one member

One-Chamber Congress

Creates Executive Committees

Foreign, Military, Indian Affairs (including making of war and peace)

Disputes between states

Financial matters (borrowing & issuing currency)

GOVERNMENT CREATED BY THE ARTICLES OF CONFEDERATION

EXECUTIVE BRANCH
President, Cabinet, and Administrative Agencies

- President approves or vetoes laws
- President heads armed forces
- President hires Cabinet officers and other chief officials
- President and Cabinet make policy
- Carries out day-to-day functions of government

LEGISLATIVE BRANCH
Congress (Senate and House of Representatives)

- Congress makes laws
- Senate approves people hired by President
- Congress approves taxes
- Senate approves treaties
- Congress declares war

JUDICIAL BRANCH
Supreme Court & Other Federal Courts

- Decides if laws are constitutional and what they mean

50 The diagram above left shows the structure of U.S. government before 1787. The government created by the Constitution of 1787 is shown on the right. Compare the two forms of government and describe at least two major differences between them.

_____

_____

_____

_____

_____

_____

_____

_____

_____

_____

II Critical Thinking Skills

Language Arts classes begin by teaching you the basics of reading and writing. Next you learn higher-order or critical thinking skills. These skills help you to interpret what you read and to express ideas when you write.

Critical thinking skills are equally important in social studies. In themselves, all the facts that have been gathered about history and geography and the other social studies are not very meaningful. Historians try to understand the causes and consequences of events. The events need to be arranged in the order in which they occurred. Information must be organized to make it more manageable and understandable. All this requires an ability to analyze, interpret, classify, and infer. These are the critical thinking skills that make social studies meaningful.

Once you have mastered critical reading and thinking skills, you must be able to express what you have learned and understood. Here, you use the writing skills you learned in languages arts classes.

As good citizens, these skills allow you to stay informed of current events. They allow you to compose letters to the editor of your local newspaper about community problems that you feel strongly about.

As social studies students, these skills allow you to understand your textbooks and to write the essays your teacher assigns.

As competent readers and writers, you will be able to:

- understand the material that is presented to you
- select from it the information you need
- rework this information so that it answers a particular question
- express this reworked information in the form of an essay

1 Reading and Interpretive Skills

Social studies require you to master many different skills. These include the obvious ones like remembering facts and understanding maps. But basic and more advanced reading skills are also essential. Unless you can understand the questions you are asked, you won't be able to answer them. Unless you can understand the social studies passages you are given to read, you won't be able to interpret them.

This chapter will take a look at these reading and interpretive skills and see how they apply to social studies. In particular it will help you to do the following:

- find a particular item of information in a text or graphic.

- describe the main idea or central purpose of a passage or graphic.

- find the details and information that support a particular idea or viewpoint.

- decide what causes and what is the result of a particular event.

- make an inference or draw a conclusion based on one or more sources of information.

- make a generalization from a conclusion you have drawn.

- work out the meaning of a word in a question or document from its context.

Finding Information in a Text

Read the passage and find the information. This is one of the easiest tasks you will be given in social studies. You simply skim through the passage until you find the information you need. It will be right there in front of you.

EXTRACT FROM STATE OF THE UNION MESSAGE TO CONGRESS

January 11, 1944

Ladies and Gentlemen:

Today I sent my Annual Message to the Congress, as required by the Constitution. It has been my custom to deliver these Annual Messages in person, and they have been broadcast to the Nation...But, like a great many other people (of my fellow countrymen), I have had the "flu" and, although I am practically recovered, my Doctor simply would not permit me to leave the White House to go up to the Capitol....

President Roosevelt in 1944

The overwhelming majority of our people have met the demands of this war with magnificent courage and a great deal of understanding...However, while the majority goes on about its great work without complaint, we all know that a noisy minority maintains an uproar, an uproar of demands for special favors for special groups. There are pests who swarm through the lobbies of the Congress and the cocktail bars of Washington, representing these special groups as opposed to the basic interests of the Nation as a whole. They have come to look upon the war primarily as a chance to make profits for themselves at the expense of their neighbors—profits in money or profits in terms of political or social preferment.

Such selfish agitation can be and is highly dangerous in wartime. It creates confusion. It damages morale. It hampers our national effort. It prolongs the war.

President Franklin D. Roosevelt

Suppose you were asked to read the passage above and answer this question:

1 **Why did President Roosevelt fail to deliver this State of the Union message in person?**

In the very first paragraph you read,

I have had the "flu" and, although I am practically recovered, my Doctor simply would not permit me to leave the White House to go up to the Capitol.

In other words, the President did not deliver his message in person because he had been ill.

Now try another question about this passage.

2 **Who are the "pests" President Roosevelt complains about in his message?**

A Foreign agitators who want to harm the war effort

B People who spend all their time having fun instead of working

C People who want special favors for the groups they represent

D Those American citizens who are opposed to the war

President Roosevelt is complaining about those "special groups" who want to make a profit out of the war. The *pests* he mentions are the people who represent these selfish Americans. Choice C is correct.

Finding the Main Idea of a Passage

The main idea or central purpose of a passage is what the passage is mostly about. If a passage has a title, the title is likely to be the main idea. Suppose you read a newspaper article headed "Powerful Hurricane Hits Miami." You would expect to learn of the destruction the hurricane caused in the city.

Often it is easy to decide on the main idea of a *short* passage or a piece of a larger passage. Suppose you were asked to read the passage below and identify the main idea of its first paragraph.

THE POPULATION EXPLOSION has led to massive deforestation. Trees have been cut down to make room for grazing and road building. In Latin America, Africa, and Asia, tropical forests are being cleared at the rate of about one percent per year.

Population pressure has also led to the loss of wetlands and the overuse of grazing areas.

Drought has made these problems far worse for the people of Sub-Saharan Africa. Several years of low rainfall have turned fertile land into desert.

Population pressure has combined with drought to increase ecological damage: rivers have been polluted, and lakes have died. It is estimated that since 1950, the world has lost one-fifth of its topsoil, one-fifth of its tropical rain forests, and tens of thousands of plant and animal species.

The first paragraph tells you that many trees have been cut down because of population growth. That is what the paragraph is mainly about. It is the main idea.

It is much tougher to decide on the main idea of this whole passage. You know the first paragraph deals with deforestation. A quick glance tells you that the second paragraph tells about the loss or misuse of other parts of the environment. The next paragraph deals with the impact of drought in Sub-Saharan Africa. The last paragraph sums up the damage caused by drought and population growth.

Now that you know what each paragraph deals with, think about what they have in common. Then decide on the main idea of the whole passage.

3 **What is the main idea of this passage?**

    A Drought has made farmland unusable through much of the world.

    B Population pressure and climate change are harming the environment.

    C Environmental change in Sub-Saharan Africa has caused the farmers in this vast region to lose their livelihoods.

    D The needs of the world's growing population and severe drought have led to massive deforestation, the loss of topsoil and grazing areas, and the extinction of thousands of species.

One of these answer choices, Choice A, is a detail from the passage. Choice C deals with just a part of the passage. Also, it exaggerates the problem by suggesting that all the farmers of Sub-Saharan Africa have been ruined. Choice D contains correct information, but it is too long. The main idea should be brief, not a rewrite of the whole passage. Choice B is correct. It tells you, *briefly*, what the whole passage is about.

Finding Supporting Details

A main idea is supported by details. The passage on the opposite page dealt mainly with population growth and its impact on the environment. Deforestation—clearing forests and using the land for other purposes—was a supporting detail.

You must identify the main idea of a passage before you can find details that support it.

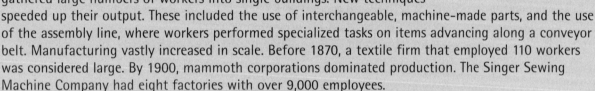

OVER THE COURSE of the nineteenth century, the industrial growth that had begun in New England's textile mills became more rapid and more widespread. Factories that had manufactured weapons, uniforms, and railroads during the Civil War now began to make goods for the peacetime economy.

Industrial growth was made possible by two factors: technological innovation and the development of the factory system. Before 1860, most manufacturing had taken place in small workshops. After 1870, manufacturers increasingly gathered large numbers of workers into single buildings. New techniques speeded up their output. These included the use of interchangeable, machine-made parts, and the use of the assembly line, where workers performed specialized tasks on items advancing along a conveyor belt. Manufacturing vastly increased in scale. Before 1870, a textile firm that employed 110 workers was considered large. By 1900, mammoth corporations dominated production. The Singer Sewing Machine Company had eight factories with over 9,000 employees.

The United States had large deposits of metals and fuels. Power drills extracted oil, gas, and water from deep within the earth. In the late 1800s, coal and iron ore from the mines of Pennsylvania, the

Great Lakes region, and West Virginia were carried by railroad to mills in Chicago and Pittsburgh. The new Bessemer process allowed them to be converted into steel quite cheaply. Finished steel was manufactured into a variety of products, from nails to rails, and from bridge beams to engines.

New equipment was also revolutionizing homes and offices. The typewriter speeded up office work. The sewing machine made clothes much faster than a pair of hands. And personal as well as business life changed forever with the invention of the telephone in 1876 and the electric light bulb in 1879.

4 **What is the main idea of the passage?**

A Industrialization spread across the United States after the Civil War.

B New inventions changed personal life.

C The Industrial Revolution began in Europe and spread to the United States.

D The United States is rich in the minerals needed for industrial growth.

The main idea is that industrialization spread across the United States after the Civil War

(Choice A). Often supporting details are examples of the main idea.

5 **Give an example from the passage that illustrates its main idea.**

_____

_____

_____

_____

_____

Using Context to Work Out Word Meanings

In 1917 Emma Goldman was tried for conspiring against the government policy of drafting troops to fight in World War I. When she spoke to the jury, she used many words that may have been unfamiliar to them. Even so, they could have worked out the meaning of most of what she said from its context.

EMMA GOLDMAN'S ADDRESS TO THE JURY DURING HER TRIAL

Emma Goldman in 1917

GENTLEMEN of the jury, whatever your verdict will be, as far as we are concerned, nothing will be changed.... Nothing on earth would ever make me change my ideas except one thing; and that is, if you will prove to me that our position is wrong, untenable, or lacking in historic fact. But never would I change my ideas because I am found guilty.

I may remind you of two great Americans, undoubtedly not unknown to you, gentlemen of the jury; Ralph Waldo Emerson and Henry David Thoreau. When Thoreau was placed in prison for refusing to pay taxes, he was visited by Ralph Waldo Emerson and Emerson said: "David, what are you doing in jail?" and Thoreau replied: "Ralph, what are you doing outside, when honest people are in jail for their ideals?"

Gentlemen of the jury...I do not wish to appeal to your passions. I do not wish to influence you by the fact that I am a woman. I have no such desires and no such designs. I take it that you are sincere enough and honest enough and brave enough to render a verdict according to your convictions, beyond the shadow of a reasonable doubt...But whatever your decision, the struggle must go on. We are but the atoms in the incessant human struggle towards the light that shines in the darkness--the ideal of economic, political and spiritual liberation of mankind!

July 9, 1917

For example, in the last paragraph she talks about the incessant human struggle towards the light. Perhaps the jury didn't know the meaning of *incessant*. But they could work it out. In the previous sentence, Goldman talked about a struggle that must go on. Now she mentions an *incessant* struggle. One could guess that *incessant* means ongoing, continuing, unending.

In the first paragraph Goldman talks about changing her ideas if they are *untenable*. Use the word's context to decide what it most likely means.

6 *Untenable* ideas are–

A   accurate

B   easy to believe

C   easy to remember

D   hard to defend

In the first paragraph, Goldman talks about what would make her change her ideas—she would change them if these ideas were proven wrong, untenable, or lacking in historical fact. She would not reject them if they were proved to be accurate, or easy to believe, or easy to remember. But if someone could convince her that her ideas were impossible to defend, then she would give them up. Choice D is the correct answer.

7 **When Thoreau talked about *ideals*, he meant–**

A   conduct

B   crimes

C   principles

D   risk-taking

Understanding Cause and Effect

Historians try to decide what was the cause of major events and what was their result. They might ask why the 13 colonies rebelled against British rule, why the North and South fought a civil war, or what was the outcome of the Union victory over the Confederacy.

Disease has had a powerful impact on human history. The Black Death was a deadly plague spread by rat fleas. Decide what made it so deadly.

THE BLACK DEATH

BETWEEN 1347 and 1350 the bubonic plague swept through Europe. The Black Death, as it was called, killed one person in three. The disease was spread by the flea carried by the black rat. When an infected flea bit a rat or a human, plague bacteria flowed into the wound.

The plague probably began in East Asia and moved westward with Mongol armies and merchants. From Russia it was spread by Genoese traders to Italy, France, Spain, England, Germany, and eventually to Greenland. Plague victims developed a raging fever with black swellings on their necks and joints. The plague is particularly deadly if people are already weak from hunger and poor diet, as was the case in fourteenth-century Europe.

Doctors were helpless because they didn't know what caused the disease. People developed their own remedies. They thought they were infected by the smell of the dead and dying and tried to ward off deadly vapors by burning incense and covering their faces with handkerchiefs dipped in aromatic oils. Another folk remedy was sound—towns rang church bells to drive the plague away.

Soon after the last outbreak of the Black Death, there was a sharp decline in the birth rate. Children were considered "not worth the trouble" to raise. It took 400 years for Europe's population to reach the level it had been before the Black Death. But some outcomes were more positive. There were now far fewer peasants to work in the fields, so those peasants who survived managed to force their lords to give them more control over their lives and land. Also, many farmworkers who left the countryside for cities were able to earn higher wages there.

8 **Why did the Black Death kill so many people?**

    A Children's lives were not thought to be worth saving.

    B Most people couldn't afford medicines.

    C No one understood how it spread.

    D There were no doctors in those days.

The problem was that no one understood that fleas spread the disease so they didn't try hard enough to isolate its victims. Now decide on one outcome of the disease.

9 **As a result of the Black Death—**

    A peasants had to work harder than ever because there were fewer of them

    B peasants won more freedom from their lords and more rights over the land they farmed

    C the cost of food, housing, and other goods increased sharply

    D the population grew because more food was now available

Making Inferences and Drawing Conclusions

When you make an inference or draw a conclusion, you have to read between the lines. Inferences are not spelled out, you must work them out based on what you know. If you read that the Black Death killed one-third of Europe's population, you could infer that the disease was very serious and easily spread.

PHILADELPHIA IN THE 1790s

BETWEEN 1790 and 1800, Philadelphia was the largest city in the United States. It was the nation's capital and its financial center. During these years the city population doubled in size, despite a series of yellow-fever epidemics that killed thousands and sent the entire federal government, including President Washington, fleeing for their lives. The population increase came from a steady stream of country folk and immigrants who poured into the city.

A Quaker merchant's Philadelphia home

National Park Service

Philadelphia society had three distinct layers. At the top were the richest 10 percent, many of them Quaker merchants, who owned half the city's wealth. Most citizens were artisans and worked in trades like carpentry, bricklaying, dress-making, and leatherwork. They supplied Philadelphia's wealthy citizens with clothes, furniture, and houses copied from European styles. These craftsmen lived fairly comfortable lives.

The lives of the "lower sort" were very different. These were the porters, dock workers, and washer women. Their work was usually temporary and always poorly paid. Poor diets and wretched housing meant that they suffered far more from disease than the rest of society and died at a younger age.

10 **What inference can you make about Philadelphia in the 1790s?**

   A   Had it not been for immigrants coming from abroad and from the countryside, the population would have declined.

   B   Most citizens were poor and found it hard to survive.

   C   President Washington lived in Philadelphia.

   D   There was great social mobility— citizens moved freely up and down the social ladder.

Choice C is not an inference; it is stated in the passage. Choice B is incorrect because you are told that most citizens were artisans and lived fairly comfortable lives. Choice D is incorrect— the passage doesn't tell you whether people could easily move from one class to another. This leaves

Choice A. You read that thousands of people were killed by yellow-fever epidemics. You can infer that the city's population might have declined but for the arrival of new citizens from abroad and from farming areas.

11 **Suppose you had read that there were more book printers and more newspapers in Philadelphia than in any other city in the nation. What conclusion might you draw?**

   A   Books were illegal in most cities.

   B   Printers and publishers belonged to the top ranks of Philadelphia society.

   C   The city was the cultural as well as the political and financial center of the nation.

   D   The poorest citizens bought many books.

Making Generalizations

Let's suppose you have concluded (correctly) that Philadelphia was the nation's cultural capital, the place for citizens to think, talk, and swap ideas. Now you want to make a generalization from this. Generalizations take conclusions and expand them to apply to more people, more places, or more situations. You might generalize that a city, anywhere in the world, that has the most book publishers and the most newspapers has to be the cultural capital of its nation.

Or you might make a generalization based on the passage about the Black Death. First, you could draw the conclusion that the main reason so many died was because of a lack of medical knowledge. Then you could generalize from this experience to all epidemics. You could say that unless doctors understand what causes a deadly disease, they cannot prevent it from spreading and killing many of its victims.

Read the passage opposite about Michigan's Upper Peninsula and draw a conclusion from it.

12 **What conclusion can you draw from this passage about living in Michigan's Upper Peninsula?**

    A Improved transportation has failed to attract residents to the U.P. because job opportunities are so scarce.

    B The area is too isolated to attract residents.

    C The Upper Peninsula has good winter skiing.

    D There are several ways that people can reach the U.P.—by ferry, by bridge, and by the roads of northern Wisconsin.

Now decide what generalization you can make on the basis of the conclusion you have drawn.

The state of Michigan is made up of two peninsulas. The Upper Peninsula or U.P. occupies one third of the state's land, but only one out of 30 Michiganians live there. It used to be hard to reach the U.P. It was separated from the rest of the state by the Straits of Mackinac, and there was no bridge across. Some travelers took a ferry across the Straits, others drove the deserted roads of northern Wisconsin to get there.

After the Mackinac Bridge was opened in 1957, travel between the two parts of Michigan became much easier. Many holiday-makers now spend their summers among the U.P.'s lakes and waterfalls. Skiers are attracted to the slopes of the Porcupine Mountains in the winter.

Even so, the population of the U.P. continues to decline. There are few jobs to hold young citizens or to attract immigrants from abroad or from the rest of the nation.

13 **What generalization can you make about population growth based on the example of Michigan's Upper Peninsula?**

    A Large construction jobs like bridge-building bring jobs to an area.

    B Many winter sports enthusiasts have moved to the Upper Peninsula because the skiing is so good.

    C Tourism declines when travel delays make it difficult to reach a holiday spot.

    D Without job growth, it is hard for a region to increase its population.

2 | Writing Skills

Writing skills are just as important as reading skills. You have learned about different kinds of writing from your language arts teachers. Some writing assignments ask you to describe your personal experiences. Others ask you to write fictional essays that tell a story.

Some kinds of writing are neither personal narrative nor fiction. They deal with the real world and real world events, past and present. These include informational essays on topics in science and social studies. Another type of non-fiction writing is the persuasive essay where you take a stand on an issue and defend your position. This chapter concentrates on informational and persuasive writing.

Handwriting, spelling, and grammar are important when you write language arts essays. They are less important in social studies. The people who mark your papers are usually told not to penalize students for spelling and grammatical errors or for sloppy handwriting. Spelling and grammar are important, but in social studies they are less important than being accurate, clear, and well-organized.

Getting Started by Using Reference Sources and Textbooks

In some ways it is much easier to write a social studies essay than a personal narrative. You are given a subject to write about—you don't have to make everything up.

Even so, you may have trouble getting started. Suppose you were asked to write an essay about the American Revolution. You might be asked:

> **Why did the colonies decide to fight for their independence?**

You need to gather information about the topic before you can begin. Where can you find it? There are two major sources of information: reference materials and your own textbooks. You can find *printed* reference materials in your school library and in public libraries. These sources include dictionaries, **encyclopedias**, and **almanacs**, where information is arranged alphabetically by subject.

If you use a computer connected to the **Internet**, then you can also use the knowledge stored on the world wide web. Select a search tool such as *Google*. You will see a box where you can type in the subject you are researching, or perhaps a name or a place.

	ENTER

After you hit **ENTER** you will see a list of websites that carry information about this topic. Click on the listing that most closely matches your topic —the closest matches are usually listed first.

GLOSSARY

encyclopedia: book with all kinds of knowledge, usually presented as articles arranged in alphabetical order

almanac: calendar of useful information in book form

Internet: a worldwide network of computers sharing and publishing information

Your social studies textbook is another important source of information. You can find information there by checking the table of contents. Or you can use the index at the back of the book where topics are listed alphabetically.

BANKS: Black Banks since 1960
BAPTISTS
BANNEKER, BENJAMIN
CIVIL RIGHTS: Cases
DISCRIMINATION: Voting
HOWARD UNIVERSITY
KING, MARTIN LUTHER, JR.
MUSIC: History and Development
NATIONAL ASSOCIATION FOR THE ADVANCEMENT OF COLORED PEOPLE
QUAKERS
SUPREME COURT
WASHINGTON, BOOKER T.

1 The information above comes from the *Encyclopedia of Black America*. Which topic would <u>most</u> likely help you write a paper on African American culture?

- **A** BANKS: Black Banks since 1960
- **B** DISCRIMINATION: Voting
- **C** KING, MARTIN LUTHER, JR.
- **D** MUSIC: History and Development

2 The table of contents in a history text contains the following chapters. Which chapter would <u>most</u> likely contain information that would help you write an essay about why the colonists fought for their independence from Britain?

- **A** Industrial Growth
- **B** Revolution and the Early National Period
- **C** The First English Colonies
- **D** Westward Expansion

The chapter in your history text entitled, "Revolution and the Early National Period" is your best choice. It is the most likely to contain information about the colonies' struggle for independence. Let's say that this is how the chapter begins:

REVOLUTION AND THE EARLY NATIONAL PERIOD

THE FRENCH AND INDIAN WAR was the last time that Britain and the colonies worked together. After this, Britain made two decisions that would damage relations with the colonists. First, it issued a proclamation forbidding them to move onto Native American lands west of the Appalachian Mountains. And second, it decided to station British troops permanently in North America to protect its huge new empire. Since the war had been costly and Britain was in debt, the colonists would pay the cost of this army.

In 1765 the British Parliament passed the first of several laws designed to raise money from its North American colonies. The Stamp Act required colonists to pay the cost of having an official stamp placed on all paper documents. This was nothing new; in Britain citizens had been paying a stamp tax for years. But British citizens had elected the Parliament that imposed this tax. Colonists had no voice in it, so Patrick Henry of Virginia objected to taxation without representation. The American protests grew bitter and the Stamp Act was repealed.

Next, Parliament passed the Townshend Acts, which taxed different kinds of goods. Again, there were angry objections from the colonists. They began to boycott British goods. British merchants were losing money and begged Parliament to repeal the acts. It repealed all the acts, except the tax on tea.

Tensions between Boston's citizens and the British troops stationed there were growing. In 1770 they exploded. A group of British soldiers fired on a taunting crowd, killing five. Colonists called the incident the "Boston Massacre" and used it as propaganda to win support for their cause.

The colonists were still angry about the tax on tea. Many people stopped drinking it, but a group of young men protested more vigorously by dressing up as Indians and dumping a shipload of tea into Boston Harbor. The British were outraged by this "Boston Tea Party." Parliament passed the Intolerable Acts, which called for closing Boston Harbor and seizing control of the government of Massachusetts.

These new laws were a severe punishment and created a split among the colonists. Those who supported Britain and its king, George III, were known as Loyalists. Those who opposed British interference were known as Patriots. Virginia's leaders wrote to the other colonies and suggested that they all meet together. The result was the first Continental Congress, which met in Philadelphia in 1774. The Congress asked the colonies to end all trade with Britain.

In Massachusetts the colonial militia had stored arms at Concord near Boston. In 1775 British troops were ordered to seize the colonists' weapons. British troops faced colonial Minutemen at Lexington and Concord. Shots were fired, and the British retreated to Boston. Later, they defeated some colonists at the battle of Bunker Hill, but their losses were severe. The Revolutionary War had begun.

This long passage contains all the information you need to write your essay. But how to begin? One good method is to underline or highlight all the sentences that help you answer the question. Take the first paragraph. You might underline as follows:

The French and Indian War was the last time that Britain and the colonies worked together. After this, Britain made two decisions that would damage relations with the colonists. First, it issued a proclamation forbidding them to move onto Native American lands west of the Appalachian Mountains. And second, it decided to station British troops permanently in North America to protect its huge new empire. Since the war had been costly and Britain was in debt, the colonists would pay the cost of this army.

Here you have three actions that troubled the colonists:

- They were banned from creating new farms in the West.
- British soldiers would be stationed in their cities.
- They would have to pay new taxes.

The rest of the passage tells you what happened when the British tried to make their new policy work. The colonists resisted, and relations between Britain and the colonists grew worse. You might want to underline some of the ways the colonists resisted and how the British reacted. You might decide that the following were important in showing how relations between the two sides worsened:

- Boston Massacre
- Boston Tea Party
- Intolerable Acts
- First Continental Congress
- British and colonial troops begin to fight

Now you have enough information to get started on your essay. A good way to begin would be to put each reason for the American Revolution into one sentence using your own words. Try doing this on the lines below.

3   **List the reasons for the American Revolution. Use one sentence per reason.**

_____

_____

_____

_____

_____

_____

_____

_____

Organizing Your Material

Once you have gathered together enough material to write an answer, you need to organize it. The diagram shows how you might do this.

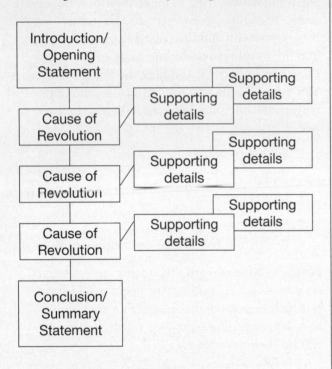

It is important to begin with an opening statement or introduction. The main purpose of your introduction is to summarize the topic you are dealing with. You could also choose to restate the question. You might begin:

> In 1776 the 13 British colonies in North America decided to fight for their independence. To understand why they did so, we need to go back in time to the French and Indian War. Before the war, Britain largely ignored its colonies. But during the war and especially after the war ended, Britain began to pay much more attention, and relations with the colonies changed for the worse. Quarrels over trade, taxes, and self-government became frequent.

You will then want to describe the major causes of the breakdown—these are the issues that you identified when you read about this topic (see the previous page). You should deal with each cause or issue in a separate paragraph. Outline the issue and give supporting details to show why it became a problem. For example, you might describe the issue of taxation like this:

> Starting in 1765 the British Parliament began taxing the North American colonies to pay for the troops it stationed there. The Stamp Act required colonists to pay for an official stamp to be placed on all documents. Following bitter protests, the Stamp Act was repealed. Next, Parliament passed the Townshend Acts, which taxed several kinds of goods. Again, there were angry objections and Parliament dropped all the taxes, except the tax on tea. Many colonists stopped drinking tea, and a group of young men dressed as Indians dumped a shipload of tea into Boston Harbor (the "Boston Tea Party").

4 Give two more reasons for the American Revolution. Use one paragraph per reason and be sure to include supporting details.

_____

_____

_____

_____

_____

_____

_____

_____

_____

_____

Once you have written the body of your essay, you must write a concluding paragraph. This is where you summarize the information you have provided and explain why it answers the question. Your conclusion might read:

The French and Indian War ended in 1763. Just 13 years later, the colonists declared their independence from Britain. These years were filled with quarrels. Some of them stemmed from the war. Britain wanted the colonists to pay for the soldiers sent to defend them—the colonists objected. Each British effort to control the colonists led to fiercer quarrels. Finally, Britain closed Boston Harbor and seized control of the government of Massachusetts. When the colonists responded to this by banning all trade with Britain, British troops prepared for war.

Editing Your Essay

When you finish writing your conclusion, you have not yet finished your essay. Your next task is to edit it. When you do this, you should ask yourself these questions:

- Have I answered all parts of the question?
- Are my facts accurate?
- Have I organized my answer clearly?
- Have I repeated myself?
- Have I expressed my ideas clearly?
- Have I strayed from the essay topic, or have I stayed on target?
- Does all the information I included deal with the topic or is some of it irrelevant?
- Have I supported my general statements with detailed information?
- Have I written an opening paragraph to introduce my topic?
- Have I written a closing paragraph to give my conclusions?
- Is my handwriting legible?

Now you will edit an answer to this essay question written by another student. As you read it, bear these points in mind.

The American Revolution began when the French Indian War ended. It was fought against the British. The colonists refused to pay taxes to the British and threw their tea into the ocean.

There were other problems, too. The British didn't want the colonists to take Native American land. This was a problem. Today it is still a problem.

Another problem was government. Americans wanted to have their own parliament and Britain wanted to keep its parliament.

The war began with the Boston Massacre in which many people were killed. The British were very angry about this.

The Stamp Tax was a famous tax on stamps and the colonists didn't want to pay it. The colonists did not want to pay any taxes.

For all these reasons the American Revolution began.

Your task will be to use the lines on the next page to rewrite this student essay. Keep the information it contains, unless the information is irrelevant or incorrect. If you think it necessary, reorganize the material to make it clearer. If statements need supporting details, add them.

5 Rewrite the student essay from the opposite page. Use the guidelines you have been given to improve its organization. You may also remove any errors and add additional material.

_____
_____
_____
_____
_____
_____
_____
_____
_____
_____
_____
_____
_____
_____
_____

Writing a Persuasive Essay

Some of the rules for writing informational essays apply to persuasive essays, too. You need to begin with an opening paragraph and end with a conclusion. You must express your ideas and organize your answer clearly. You must stay on target. And of course you must write legibly.

In other ways, persuasive essays are rather different. You will not find all the information you need in a textbook. This is because you must give your opinion, along with facts that support it.

You may be asked to write about a topic that many students feel strongly about:

- Should there be a school dress code?
- If students cheat on a test, how severely should they be punished?
- Should students be allowed to watch TV on school nights?
- Should girls' sports get equal time with boys' sports?
- What is the best way to deal with racism at school?

You will need to think and plan carefully before you begin your paper. Again, you may find a graphic organizer a good way to begin:

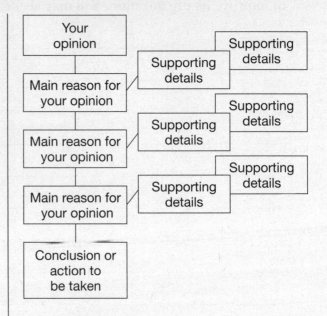

You should begin by stating your opinion about the topic. If the topic dealt with watching TV on school nights, you might begin:

> Some people think students should be banned from watching TV on school nights. They think students will not do their homework, or not do it carefully, if they can watch TV instead. I disagree. I believe it is useful and important for students to be able to watch TV every night, including school nights. In the rest of this paper I will explain why I think this.

Suppose instead that you believe that students should *not* watch TV on school nights. Write an introduction stating your point of view.

6 **Write the introductory paragraph of an essay about watching TV on school nights. Show that you are opposed to this idea.**

_____

_____

_____

_____

Now you are ready to tell your readers why you think students should or should not watch TV on school nights. Each new reason should have its own paragraph. You might write:

> I believe that students need to be able to relax after school. Watching TV is a good way to do this.

This is your opinion and it's a perfectly good opinion. But what if another student had written:

> I believe that if students watch TV, they will never get around to doing their homework.

This is an opinion, too. And it's just as valid as the first opinion. What makes one opinion more valid than another opinion? The answer is supporting facts. If you can show that your opinion is based on some kind of evidence, you are more likely to persuade your reader to agree with you.

If you are given time to prepare your persuasive essay, you may be able to do some research and find evidence to support your opinions. The evidence you find may even change your opinion!

The graph below shows how much TV 20 eighth-graders watched during one week. A month later they took a national test on reading and math. You can see how these eighth-graders did on the test.

As it happens, you could use this data to support either point of view. If you wanted to argue that students should be able to watch TV, you could write:

> Watching some TV can even help you do better on tests. A recent study showed that students who watched one or two hours of TV each night actually did better on nation-wide reading and math tests than students who watched no TV at all.

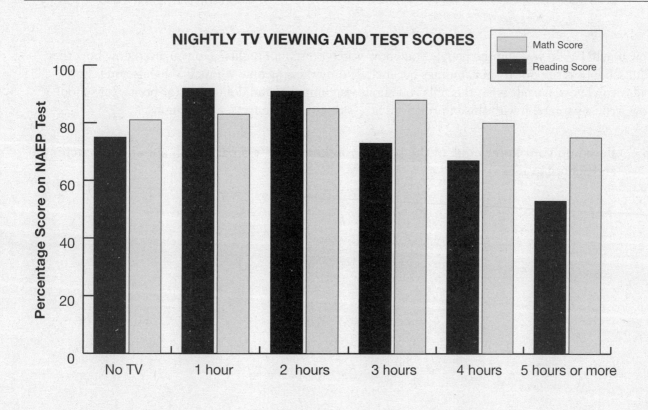

NIGHTLY TV VIEWING AND TEST SCORES

Now you can write a paragraph using this same evidence. But your task is to argue that the evidence shows that TV watching on school nights is harmful.

7 **Write a paragraph using evidence from the graph to argue that watching TV on school nights makes students do poorly on tests.**

_____

_____

_____

_____

_____

If you have to write a persuasive essay as part of a test, you will not be able to do any research. Even so, you may be able to provide some facts as well as opinions to support your position. These facts will be based on what you have seen for yourself. You may want to describe your own TV watching habits or those of your brothers, sisters, cousins, or friends. You could then describe your own or others' performance in school and find a connection. For example, you could write:

> On school nights I never watch more than an hour of TV—my parents won't let me. I'm not an A student, but I'm not failing any of my classes and mostly I get Bs. My friend Joey can watch as much TV as he wants and he watches until 11 PM most nights. He's always tired in the morning and he's lucky to get Cs.

How much TV do you and the people you know watch on school nights? Do you also know how they do in school? Write down your findings but include only those people whose TV habits and school grades you know. Decide what this tells you about watching TV and doing well (or poorly) at school. Now write a paragraph with this information. Stress that these are facts, not opinions.

8 **Based on your knowledge of the people you know, write a paragraph about TV watching and school grades.**

_____

_____

_____

_____

_____

Now you can write a complete essay. State where you stand on the issue in your first paragraph—you can choose whatever position you wish. Then write two or three paragraphs, each with a reason (fact or opinion) that supports your position. End with a closing statement summarizing your position and your supporting evidence.

9   **Should students be allowed to watch TV on school nights?**

_____

_____

_____

_____

_____

_____

_____

_____

_____

_____

_____

_____

_____

_____

_____

_____

_____

_____

_____

The Earth has warmed about 1°F in the last 100 years. The four warmest years of the 20th century all happened in the 1990s. The energy that makes cars run and much of the energy used to light and heat our homes comes from fossil fuels like coal and oil. Burning these fuels releases greenhouse gases. Many of the world's leading climatologists think that these gases are making the Earth warmer by trapping energy in the atmosphere.

Global warming refers to an average increase in the Earth's temperature. A warmer Earth may lead to changes in rainfall patterns, a rise in sea level, and a wide range of impacts on plants, wildlife, and humans. Over the last 100 years, the level of the sea has risen about 6-8 inches worldwide. When the sea level rises, the tide goes farther up the beach. Scientists think the sea has risen partly because of melting glaciers and sea ice. Scientists also think that warmer temperatures in the sea make it rise even more. Heat makes water expand—when the ocean expands, it takes up more space.

Once, all climate changes occurred naturally. Before the Industrial Revolution, human activity released very few gases into the atmosphere, but since then, through population growth, fossil fuel burning, and deforestation, we are affecting the mixture of gases in the atmosphere.

Scientists use computer programs to find out how the climate may change in the years ahead. These programs tell us that the Earth may continue to get warmer. Together, the melting glaciers, rising seas, and computer models provide good clues. They tell us that the Earth's temperature will probably continue to rise as long as we continue increasing the amount of greenhouse gases in the atmosphere.

From information released in 2000 by the U.S. Environmental Protection Agency on Global Warming

1 The average temperature of the Earth in 2003 was 60°F. What was the Earth's average temperature in 1903?

A   56°F   C   60°F

B   59°F   D   61°F

2 When did human use of energy begin to rise sharply?

F   After the Industrial Revolution

G   Before the Industrial Revolution

H   Once the glaciers began to melt and sea levels rose

J   Since the 1990s

3 What conclusion can you draw from this passage?

A   Because computer programs are able to predict climate trends, they are also able to reverse these climatic changes.

B   Farming communities are more likely to cause climate change than urban, manufacturing communities.

C   If people drove less and used non-fossil-fuel methods of heating and cooling, global warming would decline.

D   The temperature of sea water falls when the icy glaciers melt, and this causes sea levels to rise.

4 What is global warming and why do scientists believe it is the result of human activity? Use the account on the page opposite to help you write your essay.

_____

_____

_____

_____

_____

_____

_____

_____

_____

_____

_____

_____

_____

_____

_____

_____

_____

5   Automobiles burn fossil fuels and this contributes to global warming. Should private vehicles be banned from the center of large cities? Write a persuasive essay in which you argue for or against this idea.

III Test-Taking Skills

During each school year you are likely to take state reading and math tests. Perhaps you take a state social studies test every two or three years. Maybe your state gives all its students nation-wide tests every year, too. Then there are the tests that your teacher gives you in class.

Altogether, over the year, a goodly amount of your classroom time is spent in test-taking and preparing for tests. Tests are important. They help your teacher decide what grade to give you and in what areas you may need to work more. They help your school decide whether or not to promote you to the next grade or to hold you back a year. High-school students may not be able to get a diploma unless they pass certain tests.

Tests measure your knowledge and skills. Knowledge consists of the facts you learn from your lessons and the books you use. Social studies skills include the interpretation and analysis of documents and graphics. Several chapters in this book help you to learn these skills.

Test-taking is about more than specific subject knowledge and skills. You can also learn strategies that will help you do better on any test. This section walks you through the ABCs of test-taking. It starts by giving you a sense of what tests look like, the directions they give you, and how to enter your answer. You will learn how to use every bit of information you are given in the question or in the graphics that come with the question. Then you will take a look at different kinds of tests and learn how to give them your best effort.

3 Test-Taking Strategies

Following Directions

Most tests begin with written directions. These may contain information that will help you answer the questions, so read them carefully. Here is an example:

DIRECTIONS AND HINTS FOR TAKING THE SOCIAL STUDIES TEST

- Don't forget to write your name on the answer booklet.
- The test includes three kinds of questions: multiple-choice, short-answer, and essay. You must answer all types of questions.
- Read the directions carefully. Your teacher will explain anything you do not understand.
- Relax. Lots of people get nervous about tests. Just do your best.
- First, answer the questions where you know the answers. If you're not sure about an answer, skip it and then go back to answer that question later. Some questions may seem hard, but others will be easy.
- If a question asks you to read a passage, read it carefully. You may reread it as often as you like.
- Some questions will have special instructions. You may be asked:

  Use the information in the graph and your knowledge of U.S. history to answer the question.

  Use the information in the map and your knowledge of world geography to answer the question.

- Mark your answers carefully in the space provided. Do not make other marks on other parts of your booklet.
- When you are finished, double check each answer. Be sure it is the best answer to the question.

After the directions, most tests give you one or two sample questions which will not count towards your score. This gives you a feel for what the test will look like.

Pay attention to "traffic" symbols that tell you what to do next. At the bottom of each page you may see a symbol that tells you to continue or to stop, like these:

NOTICE: Photocopying any part of this book is prohibited by law.

Marking Your Answers

Not all tests are alike.

Sometimes you must mark your answers in a question booklet. This means you will use a pencil to circle or put a mark against the correct answer. (You will likely use a pencil, not a pen. You must use an eraser to change your answer.)

QUESTION BOOKLET

1 **Which amendment guarantees people the right to attend whatever church they wish?**

(A) First Amendment

B Fifth Amendment

C Sixth Amendment

D Eighth Amendment

Or you will write your answer after the question in the question booklet, using the blank lines provided.

QUESTION BOOKLET

2 **Identify an "invisible" item that was exported from Europe to the Americas. Describe the impact it had.**

_____

_____

_____

_____

_____

_____

Other times you will use an answer booklet separate from the questions that looks something like this:

ANSWER BOOKLET

1 (A) (B) (C) (D)
2 (A) (B) (C) (D)
3 (A) (B) (C) (D)
4 (A) (B) (C) (D)
5 (A) (B) (C) (D)

You use this grid to mark your answers. If you think Choice B is the correct answer for Question One, you fill in the B circle on line one.

Sometimes you must fill in an empty circle next to the letter that is the correct answer like this:

ANSWER BOOKLET

3 (A) ○ (B) ● (C) ○ (D) ○

Below is a question and a separate grid where you enter your answer. Be sure you match the question number and the answer number.

QUESTION BOOKLET

3 **The workers likely to be most productive in today's industrialized economies are those who**

A are physically strongest

B are trained in problem-solving skills

C belong to labor unions

D can work on their own

ANSWER BOOKLET

2 (A) (B) (C) (D)
3 (A) ● (C) (D)
4 (A) (B) (C) (D)

Reading and Understanding Questions

USING INFORMATION FROM THE QUESTION

Whether you are answering a multiple-choice question or an open-ended question, always begin by reading the question carefully. Underline key words. These may be instructions that tell you what to do, or concepts, or the names of people and places, issues, time periods, or other important data.

Suppose you were asked:

> **4** Explain the limits placed by the Supreme Court on newspaper writers who criticize government leaders and their policies.

You might underline like this:

> <u>Explain</u> the <u>limits</u> placed by the <u>Supreme Court</u> on <u>newspaper writers</u> who <u>criticize government leaders and their policies.</u>

<u>Explain</u>	Give the reasons for
<u>limits</u>	What you must explain
<u>Supreme Court</u>	Who is responsible
<u>newspaper writers</u>	Who is affected
<u>criticize government leaders and their policies</u>	What action is involved

Underline the key words in the next question. Choose those words that would most help you to plan your answer.

> **5** Between 1776 and 1783, the colonies fought a bitter war with Britain. The war ended in defeat for Britain and independence for the colonies. Explain this result.

Sometimes a question has information you can use in your answer. Here is an example:

> **6A** Between 1783 and 1853, the U.S. purchased, conquered, or obtained by treaty all the lands that now make up the continental United States. Describe the key events in this process.

Your clue comes from the words:

> **purchased, conquered, or obtained by treaty**

This may help you to remember the Louisiana Purchase, or the Treaty of Guadalupe Hidalgo, or the Mexican War. All these are key events in the expansion of the United States.

Now read the question again. It has been reworded slightly—otherwise it would be too easy to find the correct answer.

> **6B** Between 1783 and 1853, by buying land, by conquest, and by treaty, the nation obtained all the territories that make up the continental United States. Which of the following was a key event in this process?
>
> **A** Louisiana Purchase
> **B** Continental Congress
> **C** Civil War
> **D** Great Awakening

Of course Louisiana Purchase is the correct answer. A purchase is something you buy; the question gave you this hint.

USING CONTEXT CLUES TO WORK OUT WHAT QUESTIONS MEAN

What can you do if you read a question you don't understand? Suppose you were faced with any one of these questions.

> **7**   *Protective tariffs* **adopted by Congress in the early 1800s were warmly welcomed in Northern cities. What did these tariffs protect?**
>
> **8**   **Describe** *totalitarianism* **in Nazi Germany.**
>
> **9**   **Should the state legislature require student athletes to take** *mandatory* **tests for drugs, or should drug-testing be voluntary? Write a letter supporting or opposing this policy.**

Each question includes a term you may not know: *protective tariffs, totalitarianism, mandatory.* You must use your ability to work out the meaning of these terms from their contexts.

Question Seven tells you that *protective tariffs* were popular in Northern cities. *Northern* cities is your clue. It tells you that tariffs protected something found in places like Boston, New York, and Philadelphia, the cities of the North. We associate industry with the North, just as we associate agriculture with the South. You might guess that protective tariffs protected industry in the North against foreign manufactured goods.

Question Eight tells you that *totalitarianism* existed in Nazi Germany. Even if you don't know the meaning of this term, you probably know that Adolf Hitler was the Nazi leader. You may also know that he was an all-powerful dictator. You might conclude that totalitarianism is a political system in which the government controls political, economic, and social life.

Question Nine deals with drug-testing. You are asked to compare *mandatory* testing with voluntary testing. You know what voluntary means—doing something freely. You can guess that if testing is mandatory (as opposed to voluntary), those being tested have no choice. Student athletes are tested to see if they have used drugs, whether they agree or not.

Look at the question below. Let's assume you do not know the meaning of the word *precipitation.*

> **10**   **Which part of Africa gets the greatest amount of** *precipitation* **and which is the driest?**

How could you use context clues from other parts of the question to work out what the word *precipitation* means?

_____

_____

_____

_____

ANSWERING ALL THE PARTS OF A QUESTION

When you answer a question, be sure you answer all of it, not just a part.

> **11** **Identify the kinds of food grown in California and in the Prairies. Explain why these two regions produce different goods.**

This question has two parts: <u>identify</u> and <u>explain</u>. Read the three sample answers. Decide which answer deals with <u>both</u> parts of the question.

A California is famous for its fruits and vegetables. Corn is the main crop in the Prairies.

B California is very hilly but it is filled with valleys where there is plenty of water. Migrants from nearby Mexico provide cheap labor. The Prairies have very fertile soil, and they are very flat.

C California is famous for the fruits and vegetables grown there. The state is very hilly but it is filled with valleys with plenty of water. Fruit- and vegetable-picking take a lot of hands and migrants from nearby Mexico provide low-cost labor. Corn is the main crop in the Prairies. This region has very fertile soil and is quite flat. This makes it economical and easy to farm on a large scale and to operate the large machines needed for corn-growing.

The first answer tells what crops are grown in California and the Prairies. The second answer describes some differences between the two regions. Only the third answer answers both parts of the question. It identifies the crops grown in each region and uses geography to explain why each region is suitable for growing these particular crops.

WATCHING OUT FOR NEGATIVES

Watch out for questions that include negatives. You might be asked:

12	The Declaration of Independence met several goals. Which of the following was *not* one of these goals?

By putting the word *not* in italics, the question warns you that it uses a negative. Be sure to select the answer choice that was <u>not</u> a goal of the Declaration of Independence. In other words, when Thomas Jefferson drafted the Declaration, what was he *not* trying to achieve?

There are other terms for negatives besides *not*. Look at this question:

13	Economic developments in the Midwest before 1850 led to all of the following *except* —

Here the word *except* tells you that this is a negative question. Most of the answer choices will describe results of economic developments in the Midwest before 1850. But one will describe an outcome that was *not* a result of an economic development in the Midwest before 1850. This will be the correct answer.

Here are three questions. Underline the word in each that tells you that it is a negative question.

14	All of the following are ways of spreading cultural ideas except–
15	Which of the following is least important in traditional economies?
16	Which of these individuals never served as U.S. President?

Answering Multiple-Choice Questions

Different Kinds of Multiple-Choice Items

A multiple-choice question (also known as a selected response) might look like any of the following:

1 Unlike U.S. cabinet members, British ministers —

  A are appointed by the head of state

  B are not elected

  C are members of the legislative as well as the executive branch

  D work closely with the head of government

2 Identify the sequence in which these events occurred.

  1. Cro Magnons paint animals in European caves

  2. Homo sapiens in Africa

  3. Farming begins in Mexico

  4. The end of the last Ice Age

Which answer below lists these four events in their correct chronological order?

  A 1-2-4-3

  B 2-1-4-3

  C 3-1-2-4

  D 4-1-3-2

3 What conclusion can you draw from the graph?

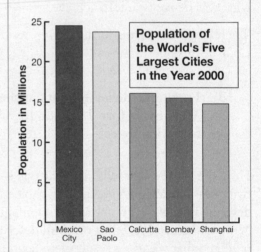

Population of the World's Five Largest Cities in the Year 2000

  A Cities are growing too fast for their governments to provide them with adequate services.

  B One quarter of the world's population lives in urban areas.

  C The populations of Latin American cities will soon equal those of Asian cities.

  D Urbanization is an important feature in some developing nations.

You can see three different kinds of multiple-choice questions on the opposite page.

Question One taps your *prior knowledge*. Prior knowledge is information you have already learned about a topic. It may be facts that you learned from a textbook or that you learned in class from your teacher. To answer this question, you need to know the difference between cabinet ministers in Britain and in the United States.

Question Two also taps your prior knowledge. You need to know what happened in early human history. But this question has a more complicated format than Question One. You have to sort the events labeled 1,2,3, and 4 into time sequence. Then you have to find the answer choice that matches this time sequence.

Unlike the other two questions, Question Three gives you a graphic to look at. In this case, you are shown a bar chart, but it could be a picture or a map, or a written passage. It is possible to answer this question without any prior knowledge. Most of the information you need to get the correct answer is right there in the graph. You will learn more about reading graphs in Chapter Eight.

To answer some questions correctly, you need to combine prior knowledge and the information in a graphic. You can see an example on the right. To answer this question correctly you need prior knowledge—the meaning of the term *opportunity cost*—and the ability to interpret the table.

The table shows how the Jackson family budgets their money. They spend $700 a month on housing, and so on. The question tells you that the Jacksons need to come up with another $200 to cover the cost of a new car. If you check the table you will see that this is exactly the amount the family saves each month. If they stopped saving, they could spend $200 more on transportation.

JACKSON FAMILY MONTHLY BUDGET

Expense	Amount
Housing	$700
Transportation	400
Food	350
Medical	350
Clothing	250
Savings	200
Other	300

4 **The Jacksons want to buy a new car. This would increase their monthly transportation costs by about $200. Their opportunity cost if they buy a new car would most likely be—**

F   their food expenses

G   their housing costs

H   their medical payments

J   their savings

As it happens, you have worked out the meaning of opportunity cost. It is the item you must do without because you choose to have something else. For the Jacksons, their savings are their opportunity cost—the item they choose to do without. Of course they could reduce by $200 the amount they spend on food, housing, clothing, or medical costs (the other answer choices). But you can guess it would be next to impossible for them to cut down on these essential expenses.

Notice the answer choices in Question Four. They are identified by the letters FGHJ, not ABCD. Some tests use different letters on the odd- and even-numbered questions. Other tests use numbers instead of letters. They label the answer choices 1,2,3, and 4.

GLOSSARY

prior knowledge: facts you have already learned about a subject

Here are some ways to improve your chances of picking the correct answer on a multiple-choice question.

Multiple-choice questions usually have four answer choices. Choose the one you think is best. Even if you are not sure of the answer, if your test has no penalty for guessing, always check off one of the choices. You have a one-in-four chance of guessing right!

Another good strategy is to eliminate the answers you know are incorrect. The next question shows you that this may be quite easy.

5 **Who was the first person to be elected President after the United States won its independence?**

   A George Washington

   B Michael Jordan

   C Queen Elizabeth II

   D Saddam Hussein

Most people know that the U.S. won its independence many years ago, so you can eliminate anyone who is living or has lived recently. You probably know enough about Michael Jordan, Queen Elizabeth II, and Saddam Hussein to eliminate them for other reasons, too. You knows that Michael Jordan is a basketball player, not a politician and Queen Elizabeth rules Britain, the nation that the colonists fought for their independence. You know that Saddam Hussein was President of Iraq until that nation was defeated in the Iraq War. This leaves George Washington. Choice A is the correct answer.

You can use the same elimination technique to answer the next question.

6 **Which of the following was U.S. President during World War II?**

   A Bill Clinton

   B Franklin D. Roosevelt

   C George Washington

   D George W. Bush

Suppose you don't know who served as President during World War II. Maybe you don't know how many years ago World War II was fought. But you do know it was fought some time ago, and of course you know that George W. Bush and Bill Clinton are very recent Presidents. You know that George Washington was our first President and lived hundreds of years ago—probably too long ago for World War II. This leaves Choice B, Franklin D. Roosevelt, as the correct answer.

Sometimes you can eliminate one or two answer choices, but you have to guess between the others. Take a look at Question Seven.

---

7 **What event first brought national fame and attention to Martin Luther King, Jr?**

    A   The Detroit race riots

    B   The first Moon landing

    C   The Montgomery Bus Boycott

    D   The San Francisco earthquake

You may not know what event first made Dr. King famous, but probably you have some knowledge of him. Perhaps you know he was a major African American leader during the Civil Rights Movement. This tells you that it was not the first moon landing or the San Francisco Earthquakes that made him famous. Now you only have to guess between the Montgomery Bus Boycott and the Detroit race riots. You have a 50-50 chance of guessing right. (The correct answer is Choice C, the Montgomery Bus Boycott.)

It is much easier to make the right guess if the question includes a graphic or passage. Question Eight includes a verse from a popular song.

Once I built a railroad
Made it run on time.
Once I built a railroad,
Now it's done —
Brother, can you spare a dime?

From the song,
"Brother, Can You Spare a Dime?"

8 **This song was written during the 1930s. What aspect of this period does the song reflect?**

    A   Industrial growth

    B   Patriotic enthusiasm

    C   Prohibition

    D   Unemployment

The question tells you that the song was written in the 1930s. If you already knew that this was a time of terrible economic depression, you could pick the correct answer immediately.

However, suppose you didn't know this. Suppose you thought the 1930s were a time of prosperity and growth and wanted to pick Choice A—industrial growth. But then, why would the verse end, "Brother can you spare a dime?" Someone who is prospering doesn't need to beg for a dime. The words of the song help you to eliminate Choices C and B, too. Alcohol was prohibited in the 1930s, but there is nothing about drink in the song. Nor does the song mention patriotism. This leaves Choice D. The singer asks for a dime because he is out of work. You can infer that someone who has to beg for a dime needs a job. The correct answer is right there in the song.

5 Answering Open-Ended Questions

Open-ended questions ask you to perform a task or to write something, as opposed to selecting the correct answer choice.
Open-ended questions come in many shapes and sizes and have many different names—open-ended questions, constructed responses, extended responses, read-think-explain questions, document-based questions, thematic essays, and so on.

We have divided these questions into three groups:

- questions that ask you to perform a task (as opposed to writing an answer)
- questions that ask you to write short answers (ranging from a word to a paragraph)
- questions that ask you to write essays of a page or more

This chapter deals with task-related questions and short-answer questions. Longer, essay-type questions will be the subject of Chapter Six.

Some questions ask you to look at a graphic or a text passage. How well you handle graphics and written documents can mean the difference between passing and failing a test. So this chapter begins with strategies for analyzing and interpreting them.

Using Information in Graphics and Text Documents

Typing class with WPA (Works Progress Administration) instructor in 1933

In later chapters you will learn more about making sense of different kinds of graphics and documents—maps, graphs, cartoons, pictures, and text passages. Here you will learn how to use graphics in answering questions.

First, it's important to look for any information that comes with a document—who created it, when, where, and for whom. The captions under and to the right of the photo above provide some of this information.

1 **What useful information do you learn about this photograph from its caption?**

_____

_____

_____

The only thing you do not learn from this caption is who took the photograph. You learn that it was taken in 1933. It shows a typing class. And it is part of the Depression and New Deal collection at the Roosevelt Presidential Library.

You may wonder why in 1933, four young men were sitting in what look like a shack, learning to type. The information that the photo is part of a collection on the Great Depression suggests the answer. The Depression was a time of economic hardship—jobs were hard to find. This helps you to answer a question like the one that follows.

2 **Use the photograph to describe one way that the federal government handled the human problems of the Great Depression.**

_____

_____

_____

_____

_____

Louisiana coastal marshes where sea levels may rise one foot every 10 years

The image shown above might be part of a question like this:

> **3** **Use this image to explain how the U.S. coastline can change.**

The image shows a coastline area surrounded by a large expanse of sea. By itself, it does not tell you very much. However, the caption contains enough information for you to answer the question.

3 **Use this image to explain how the U.S. coastline can change.**

_____

_____

_____

_____

_____

_____

Louisiana's coastal marshes are at sea level—they are part of the coastline. The caption tells you that sea levels can rise a foot in ten years. If this were to happen, parts of Louisiana's coastal marshes would be covered with water and disappear. The question asks you about the U.S. coastline. You have inferred what impact rising sea levels would have on Louisiana. You can generalize from this to make a general statement about sea levels and the U.S. coastline.

DROUGHT CONDITIONS

I have been...to see at first hand conditions in the drought states; to see how effectively Federal and local authorities are taking care of pressing problems of relief and also how they are to work together to defend the people of this country against the effects of future droughts.

I saw drought devastation in nine states. I talked with families who had lost their wheat crop, lost their corn crop, lost their livestock, lost the water in their well, lost their garden and come through to the end of the summer without one dollar of cash resources, facing a winter without feed or food -- facing a planting season without seed to put in the ground. That was the extreme case, but there are thousands and thousands of families on western farms who share the same difficulties...

President Roosevelt

First let me talk for a minute about this autumn and the coming winter. We have the option, in the case of families who need actual subsistence, of putting them on the dole or putting them to work. They do not want to go on the dole and they are one thousand percent right. We agree, therefore, that we must put them to work for a decent wage, and when we reach that decision we kill two birds with one stone, because these families will earn enough by working, not only to subsist themselves, but to buy food for their stock, and seed for next year's planting. Into this scheme of things there fit of course the government lending agencies which next year, as in the past, will help with production loans.

Fireside Chat Given by President Franklin D. Roosevelt on Sunday, September 6, 1936

Many questions include passages for you to read. Read the text above carefully and be sure to study any headings or captions.

After reading this passage, you might be asked a question something like this:

> **4** Use the passage to identify one of the problems that farmers faced in the 1930s. What kind of help did the federal government intend to provide?

Notice that this is a two-part question. The heading and the information in the first two paragraphs help you answer the first part. The information in the last paragraph tells you how President Roosevelt intends to help the farmers.

4 Use the passage to identify one of the problems that farmers faced in the 1930s. What kind of help did the federal government intend to provide?

_____

_____

_____

_____

_____

_____

_____

_____

_____

_____

Task–Related Constructed Response Questions

In a constructed response question, you perform a task such as completing a diagram or map.

There are two parts to this kind of question: the directions, which tell you what to do, and the task itself. The directions for the question below tell you to:

- use your own knowledge
- use the spaces provided to complete the diagram

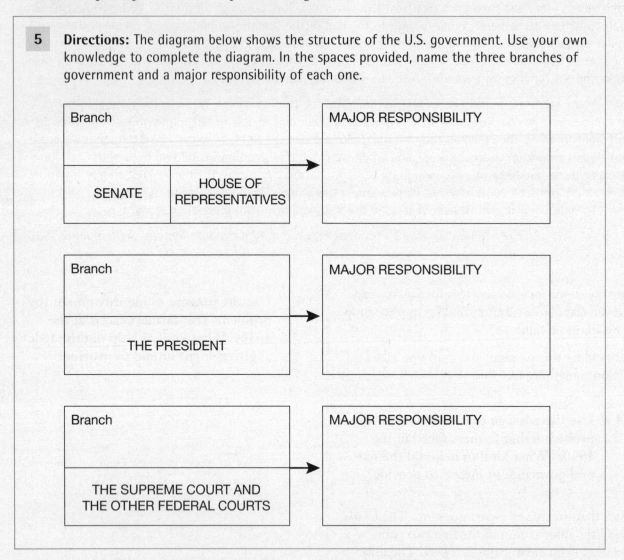

5 **Directions:** The diagram below shows the structure of the U.S. government. Use your own knowledge to complete the diagram. In the spaces provided, name the three branches of government and a major responsibility of each one.

Branch	MAJOR RESPONSIBILITY
SENATE / HOUSE OF REPRESENTATIVES →	

Branch	MAJOR RESPONSIBILITY
THE PRESIDENT →	

Branch	MAJOR RESPONSIBILITY
THE SUPREME COURT AND THE OTHER FEDERAL COURTS →	

If you were not sure of the correct answers, you would have to guess. You must be sure to answer all parts of the question by filling in all the empty spaces. You would enter the names of three branches of government where the diagram says *Branch*. Then for each branch, you would write a major function — one important thing it does—in the area to its right headed *Major Responsibility*.

Here is an example of a constructed response question that uses a map.

6 **Directions:** Label the seven continents and four oceans on this map of the world.

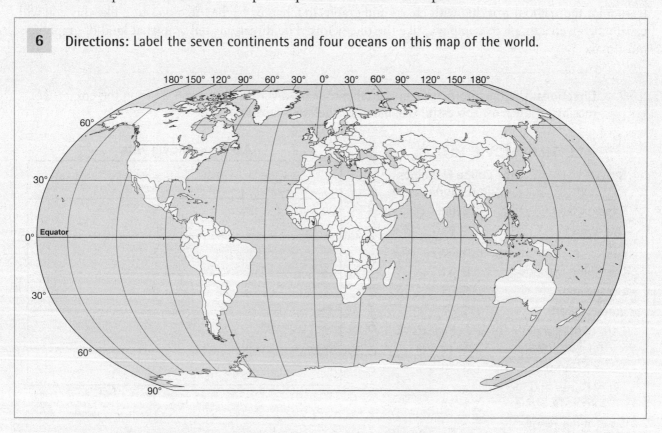

As in the diagram on the opposite page, you must use your knowledge to answer the question. Your task is to write the name of the earth's continents and oceans on the map.

In most maps, including this one, bodies of water are shaded differently from land masses—seas and oceans are usually colored darker than land. If you're certain that this is the case, you must be sure to label the oceans in the areas with darker shading.

Even if you're not sure of the names and location of *all* the continents and oceans, remember to label all the ones you *do* know.

Another task you might be asked to perform is to create a chart from information in a table. (You will learn a lot more about working with charts and graphs in Chapter Eight.) In a question like this you will usually be given a graph to complete, like the one below. The directions tell you what kind of graph you must make.

7 **Directions:** Use the information in the table to make a vertical bar graph showing the box-office receipts of the most successful U.S. movies. Label the horizontal axis.

ALL-TIME MOVIE HITS	
Movie	**Box Office Receipts (in millions)**
Titanic	$600
Star Wars	$461
E.T.	$435
Star Wars Episode 1	$431
Spider-Man	$404
Jurassic Park	$357
Lord of the Rings: The Two Towers	$338
Forrest Gump	$330
Harry Potter and the Sorcerer's Stone	$318
Lord of the Rings: The Fellowship of the Ring	$313

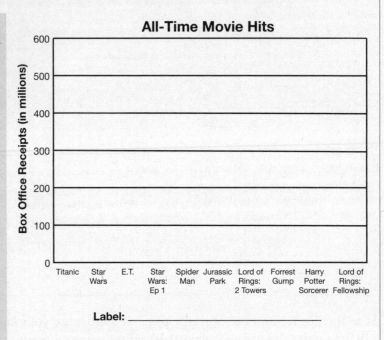

Later, in Chapter Eight, you will learn how to interpret graphs and to follow directions like these. But to give you some practice, we have created a partly completed graph. For now, your task is to add another bar to the graph on the right.

8 **Using the information in the table, add a bar to this graph to show the box-office receipts for the movie *Titanic*.**

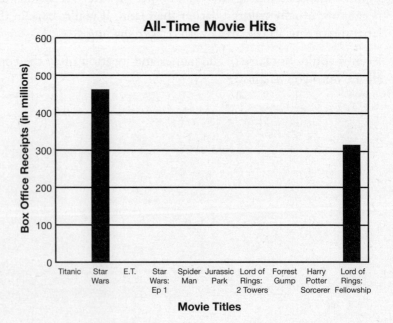

Open-Ended Questions Requiring Short Answers

A short answer may consist of a word, a paragraph, or anything in between. Usually you will be asked to look at a passage or a graphic and then asked one or more questions about it.

In this example, you are given a passage to read and then asked two questions.

> The dangers of child idleness are as great or greater than the dangers of child labor. If laws raised the minimum working age, companies would have to replace children with more expensive adults and that would reduce profits. If such child labor laws are passed, the morals of the children are going to be corrupted because they would be allowed to loaf around the street.
>
> *Statement by Southern mill owner in 1910*

9 **What argument do companies use to justify their use of child labor?**

_____

_____

_____

_____

10 **What is the true reason that companies hire children?**

_____

_____

_____

_____

Notice that you need no prior knowledge to answer these questions. The information you need is right there in the passage.

Read the passage again and answer Questions Nine and Ten.

9 **What argument do companies use to justify their use of child labor?**

_____

_____

_____

_____

_____

10 **What is the true reason that companies hire children?**

_____

_____

_____

_____

_____

POPULATION GROWTH IN 10 STATES, 1990–2000	
State	**Percentage Change**
Arizona	40%
California	14%
Florida	26%
New York	6%
New Hampshire	11%
North Dakota	1%
Ohio	5%
Oregon	20%
Texas	23%
Virginia	14%
United States	13.2%

11 Describe two factors that may explain why some states are growing faster than others.

_____

_____

_____

_____

_____

_____

12 Which states are growing more slowly than the national average?

_____

_____

_____

_____

_____

The questions on the opposite page include a table that shows population growth in ten U.S. states between 1990 and 2000. One of these questions can be answered on the basis of the information contained in the table. To answer the other question you need prior knowledge.

If you didn't have the knowledge to answer Question Eleven, you might want to tackle Question Twelve first. The graph contains all the information you need to answer this question. First you check population growth in the United States as a whole—13.2%—this tells you the national average. Then you look to see which states had a population growth of under 13.2.%

Even if you don't know the answer to Question Eleven, you can try to answer it by using your common sense. You might look for similarities among the states that gained the most population and among those that gained the least. The three biggest gainers were Arizona, Florida, and Texas. The three smallest gainers were North Dakota, Ohio, and New York. Now ask yourself what each group of states has in common. If you can find an answer, you will be able to answer the question.

Now write your answers to Questions Eleven and Twelve.

11 **Describe two factors that may explain why some states are growing faster than others.**

_____

_____

_____

_____

_____

_____

_____

12 **Which states are growing more slowly than the national average?**

_____

_____

_____

_____

6 | Answering Essay Questions

Following the Verb That Tells You What To Do

Essay questions require you to write an answer of a page or more.

A key word in the question is the verb that tells you what to do. The following verbs are often used to ask essay questions:

Compare
Show similarities and differences.

Contrast
Compare by showing differences.

Define
Explain the meaning of.

Describe
Give an account of.

Discuss
Give facts to support both sides.

Evaluate
Make a judgment taking into account information from both sides.

Explain
Make clear so that the reader knows you understand.

Trace
Follow the development of.

The paragraph below is followed by two questions.

> Totalitarianism is a system of government in which a single individual holds all power. No person or institution can check the power of this all-powerful individual.

1A **Define the meaning of** *totalitarianism.*

1B **Evaluate the advantages and disadvantages of totalitarian government**

You have learned that to *define* is to explain the meaning of. To *evaluate* is to make a judgment, taking into account information from both sides.

1 **Does the paragraph above define the meaning of** *totalitarianism* **or does it evaluate it?**

_____

_____

_____

_____

Now read three paragraphs on totalitarianism and democracy.

A In a totalitarian system, the courts of law do not protect the rights of citizens; they enforce the power of the government. In a democratic system, laws are impartial and court decisions are based on the evidence.

B Democracy began in ancient Athens. Citizens met regularly in the marketplace to decide how to run their city.

C The main advantage of democracy is that it gives power to the people. Election candidates let the voters know where they stand on major issues. Only if a majority of voters agree with their position, will they be elected. Of course, if most people fail to vote, governments may reflect the opinion of only a minority of citizens.

2 **Decide which paragraph answers the question: Compare a totalitarian and a democratic system of government.**

Choose Paragraph A, Paragraph B, or Paragraph C and write your answer below.

_____

Remember, to make a comparison, you must emphasize differences *and* similarities. In this case you must find the differences and similarities (if any) between two kinds of governments.

Now you will write a paragraph on the topic of **poverty**. Choose three verbs from the list on the page opposite. Write three short paragraphs in which you either define, or describe, or discuss, or evaluate the impact of, or explain, or trace the development of poverty, or compare or contrast poverty and wealth. Next to each question number, identify the verb you are using.

3
_____
_____
_____
_____
_____
_____

4
_____
_____
_____
_____
_____

5
_____
_____
_____
_____
_____
_____
_____

GLOSSARY

poverty: The state of being so poor as to be unable to provide for basic needs

Writing Simple Essays

The simplest essay questions give you a topic to write about. For example:

> **6** **What is *opportunity cost*? How might opportunity cost affect an ordinary American family?**

To answer a question like this you need to tap your prior knowledge of the topic. One way to begin is by brainstorming. You write down all you know about opportunity cost. You might write:

- Opportunity cost has to do with economics
- Trade-offs
- What you have to do without

You might want to create a graphic organizer to help you organize your thoughts. (You will learn more about using different kinds of graphic organizers in Chapter Seven.)

This graphic organizer gives you enough information to get started on your essay. You have defined the meaning of *opportunity cost*. This allows you to answer one part of the question. Now you must answer the second part. You must decide how opportunity cost might affect an ordinary American family.

Use the information in the graphic and whatever you know about the topic to answer the question.

6 **What is *opportunity cost*? How might opportunity cost affect an ordinary American family?**

_____

_____

_____

_____

_____

_____

_____

_____

_____

_____

_____

_____

_____

_____

Here is another essay question:

Directions: Use the illustration below to answer the question.

7   **Lady Justice is a symbol of the U.S. system of justice. As shown in the illustration above, she wears a blindfold and carries a balance scale. Explain how this symbol represents *two* characteristics of our system of justice.**

If you skim through this question, you may decide you cannot identify any characteristics of the American system of justice. But if you read the question carefully, you will find that it contains a good deal of helpful information. You learn that the blindfold on Lady Justice and the balance scale she carries are symbols, symbols of our system of justice.

Even so, you may not be sure what it means to say that a blindfold and a balance scale are symbols of justice. Your task is to work this out, rather like solving a puzzle. You could begin by asking yourself two questions:

- What happens if you wear a blindfold?
- What do you use a balance scale for?

If you are blindfolded, you cannot see. You use a balance scale to see if two things have the same weight.

Now you have to figure out how this might apply to the U.S. system of justice. If Lady Justice cannot see, she cannot distinguish among the people she is judging. If she wants the items on her scale to balance each other, she wants them to have equal weight.

Perhaps these two ideas—blind and equal—will help you recall some characteristics of U.S. justice.

Suppose you jot down:

- The law treats everyone the same.
- You cannot buy justice.
- The same law applies to rich and poor.

Use these ideas, and any others that occur to you, to write a paragraph explaining how American justice is blind and equal.

7   **The figure of a blindfolded woman carrying a balance scale is a symbol of the U.S. system of justice. Explain how this symbol represents *two* characteristics of our system of justice.**

_____

_____

_____

_____

_____

_____

_____

_____

_____

Another type of essay question asks you to examine one or more documents—these might be text passages, cartoons, maps, graphs, or other kinds of graphics. You are asked to combine information in the documents with your own knowledge of the topic when you write your essay.

Here is an essay question that uses one document:

Directions: Analyze the picture below and use the information it contains to help you answer the question.

Engraved, printed, and sold by Paul Revere, Boston

8 **The picture depicts a specific event. Describe this event and explain the role it played in the events of the period.**

The best way to get started on this question is to look at the picture very carefully. Ask yourself, What is happening? Who are the people shown in the picture? What is the setting of this event? Is there any additional information provided by the picture—a caption, a heading, a quotation, a source?

Use the lines below to list any information you find in the picture that may help you answer the question.

_____

_____

_____

_____

_____

_____

Did you include the information that this is an engraving by Paul Revere, printed in Boston? This is an important clue. If you didn't know what the picture depicts, the name of Paul Revere might jog your memory and help you work it out.

Let's suppose that you realize that this is an illustration of the Boston Massacre when British soldiers fired at unarmed citizens. This lets you answer the first part of the question. To answer the second part, you must describe the role the massacre played in starting the American Revolution. Your answer might include a paragraph like this:

> Paul Revere's engraving told the citizens of Boston what had happened. From there, news of the massacre spread swiftly through the colonies. Many colonists were convinced that the British government would use force to take away their rights. Britain was now the enemy, and more and more colonists believed they would have to fight for their freedom.

Many document-based questions include several documents. Your task is to write an essay about the topic that the documents illustrate.

The graph, photographs, and passages on this page deal with the topic of immigration. You might be asked a question like this:

9 Immigration into the U.S. increased dramatically at the end of the nineteenth century. Discuss the impact of this increase on native-born Americans, and describe what it meant for the immigrants themselves.

DOCUMENT 1

Wide open and unguarded stand our gates
And through them passes a wild, motley throng—
. . . Flying the Old World's poverty and scorn;
These bringing with them unknown gods and rites,
Those, tiger passions, here to stretch their claws.
In street and alley what strange tongues are these,
Accents of menace alien to our air,
Voices that once the Tower of Babel knew!
O Liberty, white Goddess! Is it well
To leave the gates unguarded?

from "Unguarded Gates" by
Thomas Bailey Aldrich, 1900
Protestant writer from an old American family

DOCUMENT 2

Immigrants arrive at Ellis Island
Museum of the City of New York

DOCUMENT 3

**Immigration to the
United States, 1870–1920**

DOCUMENT 4

A family living in a tenement in New York City
Museum of the City of New York

DOCUMENT 5

"See," said my father point to the flag that fluttered near,
"That flag of stars and stripes is yours;
It is the emblem of the promised land.
It means, my son, the hope of humanity.
Live for it...die for it!"
Under the open sky of my new country I swore to do so;
And every drop of blood in me will keep that vow.
I am proud of my future.
I am an American.

From "I am an American," written by
immigrant Elias Lieberman in 1916

Keep the following strategies in mind as you prepare to write a document-based essay:

- Analyze each document carefully.

- Use evidence from the documents to support your position.

- Use short quotes from text documents, and always be sure to place the quotes in quotation marks.

- Concentrate on the documents you understand best.

- Combine your prior knowledge with information in the documents in writing your essay. Some documents may help you recall your prior knowledge.

- You will need to use most of the documents in your essay to get a high score.

You may find it helpful to create a graphic organizer like the one below to sort out the information you are given. All the information here comes from the documents on Page 73.

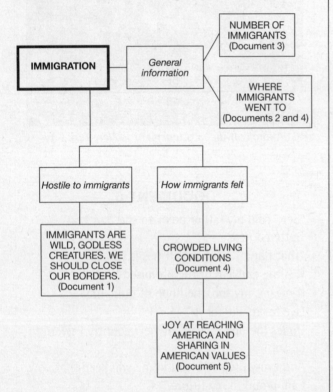

Now let's suppose you have some prior knowledge of the subject and use it to expand the graphic organizer (prior knowledge is shown in bold print):

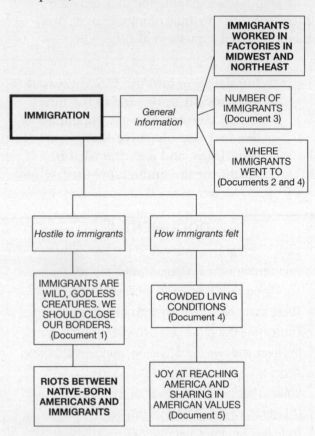

Now you are ready to write your essay. Use the information in this graphic organizer as a skeleton to help you organize your material. Your first paragraph should introduce the topic of U.S. immigration in the 1800s. A second paragraph could contain more general information on the topic. Then you can describe how opponents of immigration reacted and how life turned out for the immigrants themselves. Remember to use the strategies shown on the left.

9 Immigration into the U.S. increased dramatically at the end of the nineteenth century. Discuss the impact of this increase on native-born Americans and describe what it meant for the immigrants themselves.

Understanding Scoring Rubrics

Scoring rubrics are used to grade answers to open-ended questions, particularly essays. They assign scores ranging from a high of 5 (or 4, or 3) down to 0. For each score, they state what an essay must include to obtain this mark.

Sometimes you are shown the rubric that will be used to grade your essay. This tells you what the scorers are looking for, and what you must do to get a high mark.

Here are parts of a rubric used to mark a document-based essay. This rubric mainly measures how well the writer uses documents, taps prior knowledge to support his or her points, and structures and organizes the essay.

On the opposite page you will read a document-based essay written in answer to Question Nine. Score this essay using the scoring rubric. Use the blank lines to explain why you think the essay should be scored 5, 4, 3, 2, 1, or 0.

DOCUMENT-BASED QUESTION – SCORING RUBRIC

5
- Answers all aspects of the question by accurately analyzing and interpreting at least four of the five documents
- Includes information from the documents in the body of the essay
- Uses relevant outside information
- Richly supports the theme or problem with relevant facts, examples, and details
- Is a well-developed essay with a logical and clear plan of organization

4
- Answers all aspects of the question by accurately analyzing and interpreting at least three documents
- Incorporates information from the documents in the body of the essay
- Incorporates relevant outside information
- Includes relevant facts, examples, and details, but discussion may be more descriptive than analytical
- Is a well-developed essay, with a logical and clear plan of organization

3
- Answers most aspects of the question in a limited way, using some documents
- Incorporates some information from the documents in the body of the essay
- Incorporates limited or no relevant outside information
- Includes some facts, examples, and details, but discussion may be more descriptive than analytical
- Is a satisfactorily developed essay, demonstrating a general plan of organization

2
- Attempts to address some aspects of the question, making limited use of the documents
- Presents no relevant outside information
- Includes few facts, examples, and details; discussion restates contents of the documents
- Is a poorly organized essay, lacking focus

1
- Shows limited understanding of the question with vague, unclear references to the documents
- Presents no relevant outside information
- Includes little or no accurate or relevant facts, details, or examples
- Attempts to complete the question, but demonstrates a major weakness in organization

0
- Fails to address the question, is illegible, or is a blank paper

9 **Immigration into the U.S. increased dramatically at the end of the nineteenth century. Discuss the impact of this increase on native-born Americans, and describe what it meant for the immigrants themselves.**

During the late 1800s and the early 1900s many people came to this country from other parts of the world. The new immigrants had to adjust to their life here and the native born Americans had to respond to the new people.

Immigration consisted on average of several hundred thousand people a year between 1870 and 1900. Then in the next twenty years it increased even more. According to document 3, there were three or four times as many immigrants between 1900 and 1920 as there were in the years before. The potato crop failed in Ireland and many people there starved so this was one reason many people there and in other places came to the USA.

Many people came through Ellis Island. Document 2 shows large numbers of people arriving. The new immigrants often went to big cities. Many stayed in NYC where large numbers of people might live together in one room. Document 4 shows a family with 3 or 4 kids living in NYC in a tenement house which is a building that contains many families in small rooms. These people didn't speak English so many took jobs in factories where they worked long hours for little pay. They worked in many jobs like selling clothes door to door. Many people from Ireland became policeman. The immigrants needed work and they were willing to work at many difficult jobs.

The native born citizens didn't like competing with hard working people who accepted little pay. They wanted to keep all the best jobs for themselves. They didn't want the newcomers to have citizenship and the right to vote. Document 1 shows that some American-born citizens were afraid of the newcomers. They didn't like the fact that they spoke foreign languages.

People who came to America acted in different ways. There is a movie now about the gangs of New York that shows that a lot of immigrants joined gangs. But most didn't. Document 5 shows how most immigrants felt. They often just were proud to be American. They wanted to feel the freedom of America and they were willing to work hard for it.

America needs immigrants. There is a poem written on the Statue of Liberty which says America is a place of freedom for all people including the poor.

Using the rubric opposite, score this essay. Give it a score between 0 and 5 _____

Explain why you think this is the correct score. _____

_____

Now reread your own essay on the same topic (on page 75) and use the rubric to give it a score.

_____

Unit Review

1 **Directions:** The table below shows how Britain's actions before the American Revolution led to ever stronger responses from the colonists. Use the information in the passage on page 34 to complete the table. In the spaces provided, identify a British action or the colonists' response.

STEPS TO REVOLUTION

Date	British Action	Colonists' Response
1763		Anger; some ignore Proclamation and settle in Ohio Valley
1765	Stamp Act taxes colonists to pay for British troops stationed in North America	Formal protest; boycott of British
1766	Stamp Act repealed	End of boycott
1767	Townshend Acts tax imported glass, paper, tea; Writs of Assistance to prevent smuggling	Boston Massacre (colonists riot; five men killed by British troops)
1770	Townshend Acts repealed for all goods except tea	
1773	Tea Act gives East India Company a monopoly on tea trade	
1774		First Continental Congress asks colonies to ignore new acts and organizes trade ban, sends grievances to Parliament; colonies start training soldiers

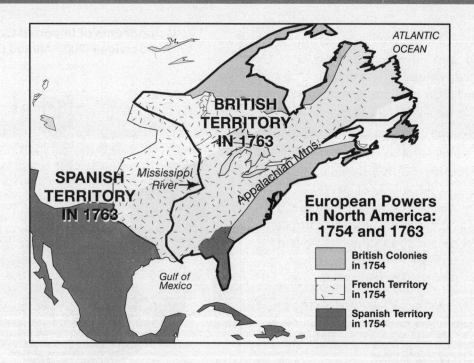

Map: European Powers in North America: 1754 and 1763

- British Colonies in 1754
- French Territory in 1754
- Spanish Territory in 1754

Labels on map: ATLANTIC OCEAN, BRITISH TERRITORY IN 1763, SPANISH TERRITORY IN 1763, Mississippi River, Appalachian Mtns., Gulf of Mexico

2 Use the information in the map above to explain how the 1754 boundaries of European empires in North America changed when the French and Indian War ended in 1763.

_____

_____

_____

_____

_____

_____

_____

_____

_____

_____

_____

_____

_____

_____

_____

Hostility between North and South was made worse by pro- and anti-slavery violence in Kansas ("Bloody Kansas," it was called). President Buchanan tried unsuccessfully to make peace between the two sides.

This was followed by an overwhelming public response to the publication of *Uncle Tom's Cabin*, a sentimental and heart-rending fictional account of the horrors of slavery. Feelings were whipped up still more by the Supreme Court decision in the Dred Scott case. The Court declared it unconstitutional to ban slavery in the territories. Then in 1859, John Brown tried to lead an armed slave uprising.

North-South tensions reached fever pitch when Abraham Lincoln was elected President in 1860. Southern states feared he would try to abolish slavery everywhere.

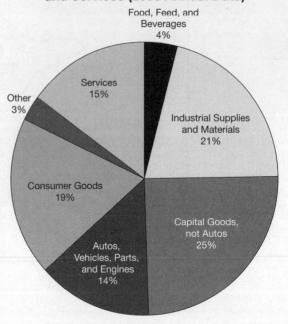

Components of Imported Goods and Services (2000 Annual Data)

3 **Identify the sequence of events before the Civil War.**

1 Dred Scott decision

2 Abraham Lincoln elected U. S. President

3 Publication of *Uncle Tom's Cabin*

4 John Brown's uprising

Which answer below lists the events in their correct chronological order?

A 1, 2, 4, 3

B 2, 1, 4, 2

C 3, 1, 4, 2

D 4, 1, 3, 2

4 **Use the passage above to decide which of the following events was *least* important in the outbreak of the Civil War.**

F The activities of President Buchanan

G The *Dred Scott* decision

H The election of President Lincoln

J The publication of *Uncle Tom's Cabin*

5 **The chart above shows the goods and services that the United States imported in 2000. Use your test-taking skills to decide which of the following are *capital goods*.**

A Aircraft, semiconductors, computer parts, engines and other machinery used to produce finished goods

B Consumer items

C Services

D Unprocessed foodstuffs such as grains and cattle

6 **What conclusion can you draw from the chart?**

F Automobiles and auto parts are imported largely from Japan.

G Over one half of U.S. imports consist of consumer goods such as clothing and household appliances.

H The United States exports more goods than it imports.

J The United States produces most of the food it needs.

IV Interpreting Graphics

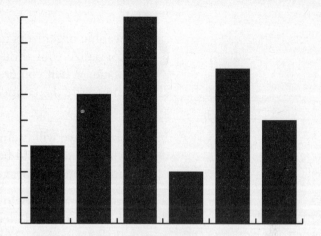

ost of the graphics found in social studies texts and on social studies tests belong to one of four groups. The first group consists of graphs, charts, and tables. Pictures in the form of paintings, drawings, cartoons, and photographs form another group. Maps of all kinds make up a third group. The fourth group consists of graphic organizers—diagrams used to show the structure or sequence of events.

It's fairly easy to make sense of some kinds of graphics—photographs, for example. Others like line graphs or graphic organizers are not so simple, and you have to learn how to read them. Even with pictures, it is easy to miss important information they may contain, perhaps in their captions.

This section shows you many examples of all four kinds of graphics and gives you tips on how to analyze and interpret them.

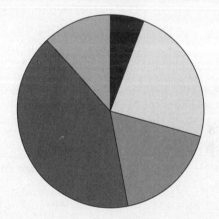

7 Graphic Organizers

Graphic organizers (also known as semantic maps) can help you to organize your thoughts when you write an essay or analyze a passage. When you create an organizer from a written passage, it allows you to see the connections between different parts of the text in a single glance.

In this chapter we will examine different kinds of graphic organizers and decide which kind should be used for what purpose. Below you can see four of the most often used organizers.

The graphic organizer below left is used to illustrate the main idea and the details that support this idea. The main idea is placed in the circle at the center of the organizer. The circles that hang off the center circle contain supporting details. The organizer below right shows the sequence in which events occur. The earliest event is placed in the oval at the top left. To the lower left of this is an organizer that shows cause and effect. At the bottom right is a Venn diagram, which is used to compare people, places, events, or ideas.

You will learn more about each of these graphic organizers in the pages that follow.

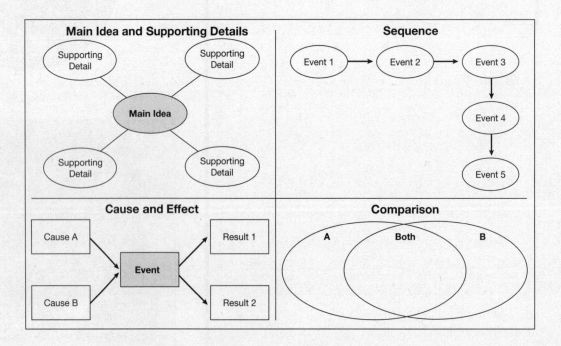

Graphics That Show Main Idea and Supporting Details

Read this passage in which John Adams, who became the second U.S. President, tells his daughter what kind of man she should marry.

The organizer below the text passage illustrates Adams' views. In the center is the main idea—the ideal husband. The surrounding circles contain qualities that Adams believed the ideal husband must possess.

> Daughter! Get you an honest man for a husband, and keep him honest. No matter whether he is rich, provided he be independent. Regard the honor and moral character of the man more than all other circumstances. Think of no other greatness but that of the soul, no other riches but those of the heart. An honest, sensible, human man...laboring to do good rather than be rich, to be useful rather than make a show, living in modest simplicity clearly within his means and free from debt and obligations, is really the most respectable man in society...
>
> *John Adams, letter to daughter*
> *Abigail Adams*
> *April 8, 1783*

Notice that when you create a graphic organizer you often need to find a brief way of summarizing ideas. John Adams doesn't use the term "ideal husband," but that is what he is describing.

Now read another passage and then complete the organizer that follows.

> The buffalo provided the people of the Great Plains with food, shelter, tools, and clothing. They ate its meat. They used its hide for tipis, for shields, and as robes. The animals' sinews were made into bowstrings. Its bones were used to fashion hoes, knives, and fishhooks. They even used its skull in their ceremonial Sun Dance.

You will need to decide on the main idea of the passage and put this in the shaded oval. Then you must find three supporting details. A fourth supporting detail—tools—has been placed to start you off. You must also find three examples of tools for the ovals that surround this one.

1 Use the information in the passage to complete the graphic organizer.

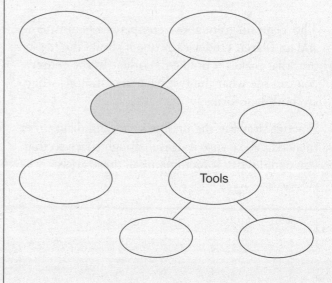

Venn Diagrams for Making Comparisons

A Venn diagram helps you to see how people or things or places differ and also how they are alike.

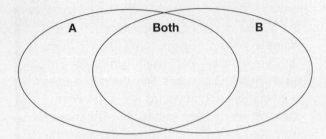

Venn diagrams consist of two overlapping circles or ovals. Where the circles overlap you write what the people or things being compared have in common. Those parts of the circles that don't overlap are where you write their differences.

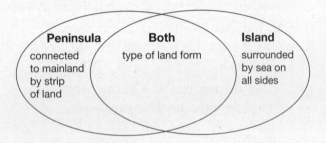

The Venn diagram above compares a peninsula and an island. Under each one it shows the feature that makes it unlike the other. In the center you can see what the two have in common—they are both landforms.

Practice drawing the outline of a Venn diagram in this box. Make sure to leave enough space so that you could write something in all three areas.

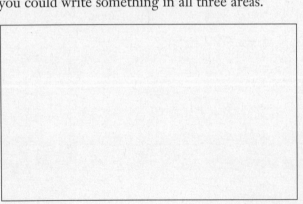

A Venn diagram is a useful tool when you have to write an essay where you compare two things. Suppose you have been asked:

> **2** **The United States is the richest nation in the world and Africa's Democratic Republic of Congo is one of the poorest. Compare the economies of the two nations.**

You might start by jotting down some features of the U.S. and Congolese economies.

United States	Congo
Technology (railroads, bridges, etc.)	Little industry
	Few modern cities Small population
Skilled workers	Most workers are poor farmers
Investment capital	No investment capital—must borrow money

If you put your notes into a Venn diagram, you might come up with something like this:

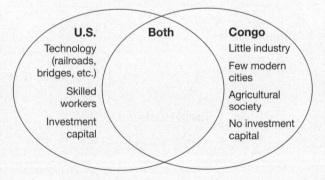

When you make comparisons, look for similarities as well as differences. One thing that makes a nation wealthy is its resources. The United States is rich in mineral resources like oil, coal, iron, and natural gas, and it has millions of acres of fertile farmland. Congo is also rich in minerals like copper, gold, silver, and diamonds. It has deposits of oil offshore. Its soil is rich, and it has large tropical forests with valuable wood.

2   **The United States is the richest nation in the world and Africa's Democratic Republic of Congo is one of the poorest. Complete the diagram by showing what these two economies have in common.**

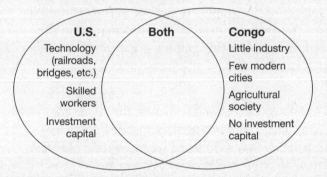

The passage on the right describes some strengths and weaknesses of the two sides in the American Revolutionary War. Use it to create a Venn diagram in the space below.

The British had a well-trained, professional army and navy. The colonists had neither; their troops were poorly trained and equipped, and often unpaid. Even so, the colonists won a stunning victory in the war.

There were several military reasons for this. British fighting tactics were often useless in the wooded, hilly land where many of the battles were fought. It was difficult and expensive to send troops and supplies 3,500 miles across the ocean, and British taxpayers were increasingly reluctant to foot the bill. Also, once France began to support the colonists, Britain had to fight a war in the Caribbean as well as North America.

George Washington was patient and stubborn—just the right kind of general to lead colonial troops. He realized that his Continental Army must be able to fight and win formal battles if they were to defeat the British. British troops had a tradition of bravery under fire. Colonial soldiers needed to develop the same discipline and nerve, so Washington hired Baron von Steuben to get them into shape.

But the colonists won mainly because they were fighting for their land and their ideals. Most British troops were mercenary soldiers, hired to fight. The Patriots believed they were fighting a revolution against oppression and wanted to govern themselves.

3   **Use the information in the passage to complete the diagram. Show the differences and similarities (if any) between the two sides in the Revolutionary War.**

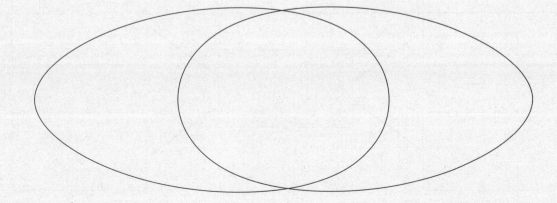

Graphic Organizers That Show Cause and Effect

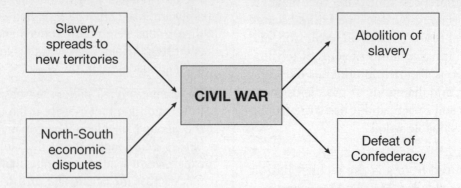

Major events can be easier to understand if you put them into graphic organizers. The organizer above is very over-simplified, but it does give the big picture of the Civil War. Historical events particularly lend themselves to this kind of treatment—much of history is a study of causes and consequences.

Read the passage below and complete the organizer at the bottom of the page. This time your task is to find the origins and results of feudalism. Identify the subject of the graphic organizer in the central box and place its causes and effects in the surrounding boxes. You will not need all the information in the passage. Sort through the text and decide what you need to complete this graphic organizer. Remember to find a way to summarize each item before you enter it in a box.

The fall of the Roman Empire was followed in Western Europe by a period known as the "Dark Ages." Cities and roads decayed, trade declined, as did law and order, and barter replaced money. The invasions that destroyed Rome were followed by more destruction. Arabs attacked southern Italy, Magyars stormed through Central Europe, and Scandinavian Vikings conquered many coastal areas.

Communities were cut off from their neighbors and left to fend for themselves. A political system known as feudalism evolved to deal with this situation. It was based on a grant of land in return for military service. Kings gave estates to their vassals (nobles). In return, vassals promised to provide soldiers to fight for the king. This arrangement tended to weaken the power of the king and to strengthen that of the greater nobles.

4 Use the information in the passage about the origins of feudalism to complete the diagram.

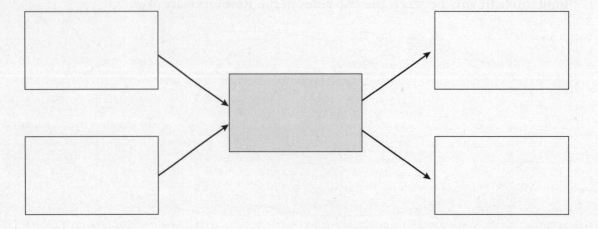

Graphic Organizers That Show Sequence

A fourth kind of graphic organizer can be used to show the order in which events occur. Here is a simple example:

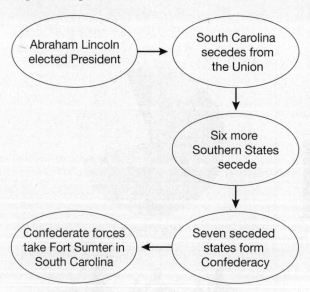

Each event is followed by the event to which the arrow points. An event may cause the event that follows it, but this need not be the case.

Organizers may show several sequences of events. In the graphic below you can see two sequences of events that followed the Civil War.

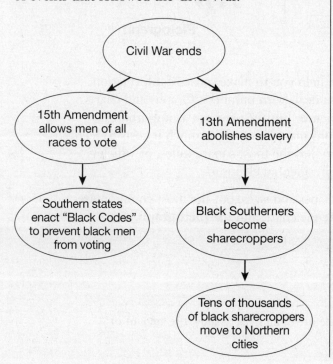

Use the space below to create a graphic organizer. Include the following events which are shown in no particular order:

- Britain creates a new empire in India
- George W. Bush becomes President
- Union and Confederate forces fight Civil War
- Colonists defeat Britain and win their independence in American Revolutionary War
- Britain creates 13 colonies in North America
- India wins its independence from Britain

Decide whether to show this information as one long sequence, or to create more than one chain of events as in the graphic at the bottom left.

5 **Place the events listed above in a graphic organizer to show their sequence.**

8 | Graphs, Charts, and Tables

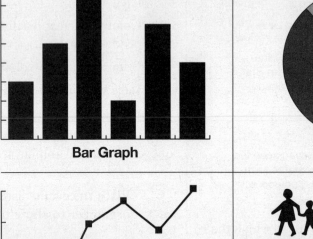

Bar Graph

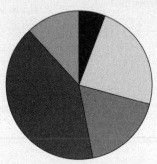

Pie Chart

Line Graph

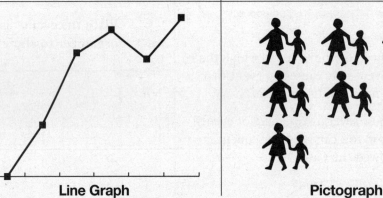

Pictograph

Graphs, charts, and tables help you to make sense of information. Most of this information deals with numbers. Graphs and charts are used in math and science. But they are just as important in social studies. Social studies graphs may tell you how much it costs to feed a family of four, or which country has the most square miles, or which group casts the most votes in a presidential election.

Graphs and charts come in all shapes and sizes, but the most common are the bar graph, the line graph, the pie chart, and the **pictograph**.

GLOSSARY

pictograph: a graph that uses a picture of an item to show the amount of the item.

NOTICE: Photocopying any part of this book is prohibited by law.

Bar Graphs

Like other kinds of graphs, bar graphs tell you about quantities—how many states, how much steel, for how many years, and so on. Each bar represents a particular unit. In the graph below, each bar represents a state.

The different parts of this bar graph are labeled. The title is a summary of what the graph shows. The **horizontal axis** at the bottom of the graph tells you more about what is being measured. In this case, it identifies the six U.S. states with the smallest populations. The **vertical axis** is usually at the left of the graph. It shows the amounts or quantities being measured. In this case, we are measuring the number of people in a state.

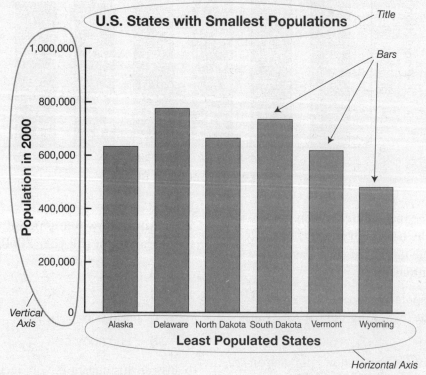

This bar graph helps you see at a glance which state has the most people and which has the fewest. Notice that it does not tell you *exactly* how many people live in these six states. Use the numbers on the vertical axis to decide *roughly* how many people each state contains.

1 **Which state in the graph has the largest population?**

   A   Alaska

   B   Delaware

   C   North Dakota

   D   South Dakota

To answer this question you simply look to see which bar is the tallest. The answer is Delaware, so Choice B is correct. If you want to know about how many people live in Delaware, place a ruler at the top of Delaware's bar. The ruler hits the vertical axis just below the figure 800,000. This tells you that Delaware's population is about 780,000.

GLOSSARY

horizontal axis: the line at the bottom of a graph that identifies items being measured or time in years, months, etc.

vertical axis: the line at the side, usually the left side, of a graph that identifies amounts

U.S. States with Smallest Populations in 2000

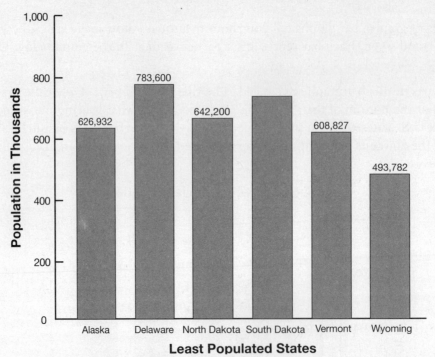

Tests and texts have many different ways of showing bar graphs. The bar graph above is basically the same as the one on the previous page, but with two important changes.

First, the exact population size is now given at the top of each bar (excepting the bar for South Dakota).

Second, the vertical axis now shows population figures in the thousands. Here's what this means:

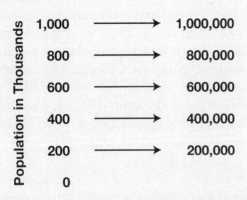

2   **About how many people lived in South Dakota in the year 2000?**

A   750

B   800

C   750,000

D   800,000

To answer this question, you need to find the top of the bar for South Dakota and then look for the numbers level with this on the vertical axis. South Dakota's population lies between the numbers shown as 600 and 800, but closer to 800, say 750. If you add three zeros you get 750,000.

3   **Which state has a population of 642,200?**

A   Alaska

B   North Dakota

C   South Dakota

D   Vermont

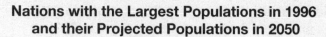

Nations with the Largest Populations in 1996 and their Projected Populations in 2050

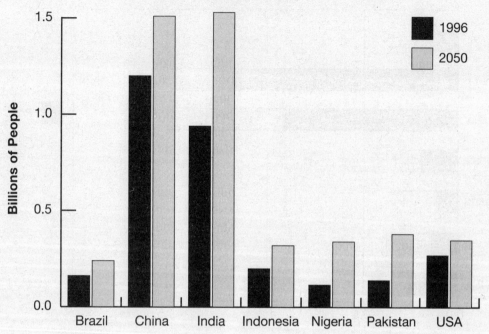

The previous bar graphs showed historical data—information that is known to be accurate because it has already happened and been measured. This bar graph shows **projected** data—information about the future that experts believe *will* be accurate.

Again, the graph deals with population size, this time the size of the world's largest populations. It shows how many people lived in the seven most highly populated nations in 1996 and how many people are expected to live there in 2050.

The vertical axis shows population figures in the billions. The number 1.5 stands for one and a half billion people, the number 1.0 stands for a billion people, and so on. (Remember that a billion is a thousand million.)

The horizontal axis identifies seven nations. For each one, the black bar shows the population in 1996 and the grey bar shows how large the population is projected to be in 2050.

GLOSSARY

projected: what is expected in the future, based on data available today

4 **What size is the U.S. population projected to be in 2050?**

A   36,000,000

B   360,000,000

C   3,600,000,000

D   36,000,000,000

The answer depends on the height of the grey United States bar. The number on the vertical axis opposite the top of this bar is something between 0 and .5, say .36. If you multiply .36 by one billion (remember the scale is in billions), you obtain 360,000,000.

5 **Which nation will add the most people between 1996 and 2050?**

A   China

B   India

C   Indonesia

D   Pakistan

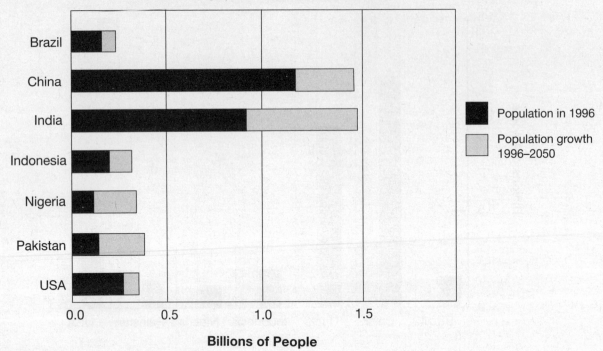

Nations with the Largest Populations in 1996 and their Projected Populations in 2050

Brazil
China
India
Indonesia
Nigeria
Pakistan
USA

0.0   0.5   1.0   1.5

Billions of People

■ Population in 1996
▨ Population growth 1996–2050

It is important to be familiar with the different ways that bar graphs are presented. This bar graph contains the same information as the one previous, but it looks quite different.

The bars are horizontal instead of vertical. And each nation is represented by only one bar. The darker part of each bar shows population size in 1996. The lighter part shows population growth between 1996 and 2050.

This means you have to add together both parts of a bar to obtain the projected populations for 2050. Suppose you were asked Question Four again:

> **4** **What size is the U.S. population projected to be in 2050?**

The U.S. population in 1996 (the black portion of the bar) was about three hundred million or 300,000,000. The population was projected to grow by about sixty million (the gray portion of the bar) between 1996 and 2050. This means that the projected population in 2050 is 360,000,000.

6 **What is the projected size of the population of China in 2050?**

A   About 90,000,000

B   About 900,000,000

C   Nearly 1.5 billion

D   About nine billion

7 **By about how much will the population of India increase between 1996 and 2050?**

A   Half a million

B   Half a billion

C   1.4 billion

D   1.5 billion

Line Graphs

Line graphs show how quantities change over time. Like bar graphs, the vertical axis usually shows quantities. The horizontal axis shows time, usually in years.

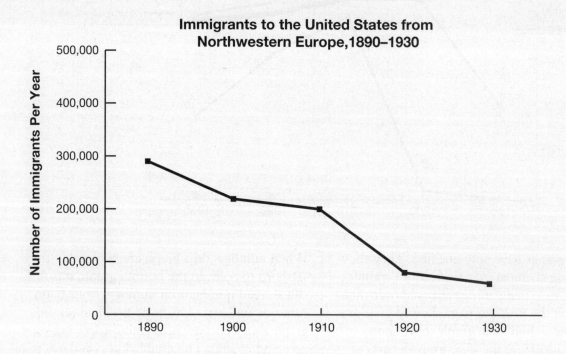

Immigrants to the United States from Northwestern Europe,1890–1930

The graph above shows the number of immigrants who came to the United States from northwestern Europe. Like most line graphs, the title includes the time period covered, in this case, 1890–1930.

Each dot on the graph corresponds to the year below. The dot above 1890 tells you that about 300,000 immigrants arrived from Northwestern Europe that year. A continuous line joins the dots together.

Notice the steep decline in immigration between 1910 and 1920. World War I was fought during this period. Many men died in the fighting. Then in 1918 there was a deadly outbreak of influenza. It took a long time for European families to recover from the losses and misery of these years and get moving again.

8 **About how many northwestern Europeans immigrated to the United States in 1900?**

A   100,000

B   210,000

C   290,000

D   Half a million

9 **By about how much did immigration from northwestern Europe decline between 1890 and 1930? That is, how many fewer immigrants were there in 1930 than in 1890?**

A   About 50,000

B   About 100,000

C   About 200,000

D   About 300,000

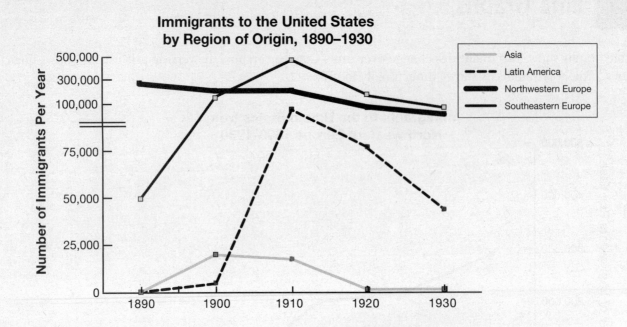

Immigrants to the United States by Region of Origin, 1890–1930

Legend:
- Asia
- Latin America
- Northwestern Europe
- Southeastern Europe

Simple line graphs have only one line. They show how one thing changed over time. More complex graphs show how many things changed over time. The graph on the previous page showed immigration from one region. The graph above shows how immigration into the U.S. from all parts of the world changed between 1890 and 1930.

Notice the numbers on the vertical axis. In the previous graph, these numbers are regularly spaced in intervals of 100,000. On this graph, the intervals are irregular. Starting from the top, they begin with intervals of 200,000 and then change to intervals of 25,000. You will understand the reason for this if you look at the graph below.

When numbers on a graph are very small, they are hard to read. In the bottom graph, it is difficult to read immigration numbers from Latin America and Asia. This is no problem on the graph above because it has more space between zero and 25,000. The double lines on the vertical axis alert you that the amount of space between numbers has changed.

10 After which year did the number of immigrants from Southeastern Europe overtake the number from Northwestern Europe?

A 1890

B 1900

C 1910

D 1920

11 Which region provided the greatest number of new immigrants between 1900 and 1910? (Be careful how you answer this.)

A Asia

B Latin America

C Northwestern Europe

D Southeastern Europe

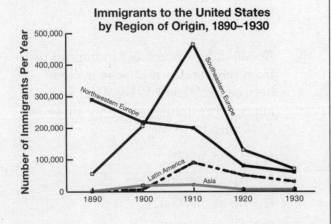

Immigrants to the United States by Region of Origin, 1890–1930

Pie Charts

Pie charts are used to show **relative** amounts of a single whole. For example, a pie chart might show how much of its income a family spends on food, housing, clothes, medical care, transportation, and other expenses. It does this by dividing a circle into slices. Each slice of the pie represents a different kind of family expense. Pie charts are easy to understand—you can tell at a glance which categories are larger and which are smaller.

Geographical Size of the Thirteen British Colonies

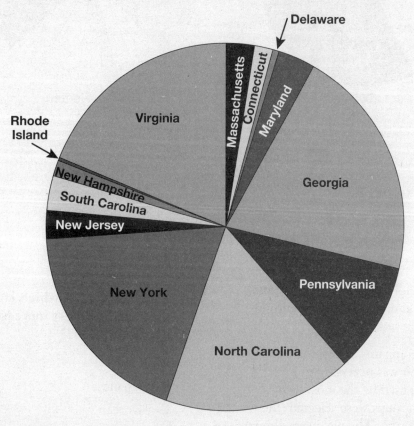

Unlike bar graphs and line graphs, pie charts do not have a vertical axis to show amounts. Some pie charts do include numbers. (See, for example, the pie chart on page 97.) In others, you must decide on size by eyeballing the pie chart.

In the pie chart above, the whole pie represents the total size of the 13 British colonies. Each slice represents one colony.

GLOSSARY

relative: measuring an item by comparing it with other items rather than in terms of its actual value

12 **Which four colonies were more or less the same size?**

A   Georgia, Maryland, Pennsylvania, and South Carolina

B   Georgia, New York, North Carolina, and Virginia

C   Massachusetts, Connecticut, Maryland, and New York

D   Rhode Island, Delaware, New Jersey, and Pennsylvania

Nine Language Groups With Most Internet Usage

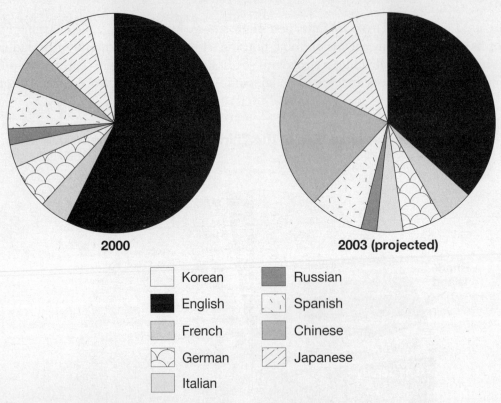

2000   2003 (projected)

☐	Korean	▨	Russian
■	English	⊡	Spanish
▨	French	▨	Chinese
⊕	German	▧	Japanese
▨	Italian		

A single pie chart cannot show change over time. To show information at different dates, multiple pie charts are used.

The pie chart above compares internet use in 2000 and 2003. First, it was necessary to find which languages were used by the most web users. Nine language groups were selected (they are listed below the charts). The pie charts shows the amount of internet time logged by speakers of these nine languages. As you can see, English speakers were far and away the biggest users in 2000. However, their share was projected to decline by 2003.

13 **The speakers of which language were projected to _most_ increase their internet use by 2003?**

A   Chinese

B   Japanese

C   Korean

D   Spanish

Making Charts from Tables

Facts and figures are often shown in tables like the one below. It can take time to grasp information when it is presented in this way. That is why the information in tables is often transferred to pie charts.

U.S. Population by Race or Hispanic/Latino Origin, 2000

Race	Number	Percent
White	194,552,774	69.1
Hispanic/Latino	35,365,818	12.5
African American	33,947,837	12.1
Asian	10,123,169	3.6
American Indian/ Alaska Native	2,068,883	0.7
Native Hawaiian or Other Pacific Islander	353,509	0.1
Mixed or Other	5,069,916	1.8

Most of the information in the table on the left has been entered in the pie chart below it. Notice that this pie chart, unlike those on the previous pages, does include numbers. These show the total U.S. population broken into percentages according to racial grouping.

14 **What information does the table, but *not* the pie chart, include?**

A Exactly how many members of each racial group live in the United States

B The average age of members of U.S. racial groups

C The names of the different racial groups that make up the U.S. population

D The percentages of each racial group in the U.S. population

15 **Which group is the second largest?**

A African Americans

B Asian Americans

C Hispanic Americans

D Native Americans

U.S. Population by Race or Hispanic/Latino Origin, 2000

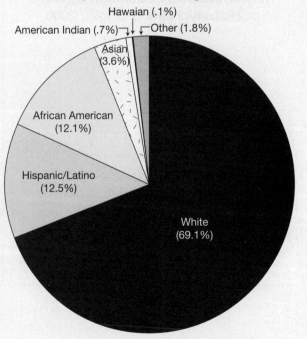

Pictographs

Pictographs are used to show quantities of an item. They use symbols or pictures to represent the item, rather than bars or lines or pie slices. Like pie charts, pictographs are easy to understand at a glance.

The pictograph below deals with cotton; its symbol is a cotton plant. Each symbol represents 1,000 tons of cotton. Suppose you were asked how many tons of cotton the United States exported in 1800. The pictograph shows only half a cotton symbol for that year. This tells you that the United States exported half of 1,000 tons—500 tons—in 1800.

Cotton Exports, 1820–1860

(🌿 = 1,000 tons of cotton)

1800　🌿

1820　🌿 🌿 🌿 🌿 🌿

1840　🌿 🌿 🌿 🌿 🌿 🌿 🌿

1860　🌿 🌿 🌿 🌿 🌿 🌿 🌿 🌿

---

16 **How many tons of cotton did the U.S. export in 1860?**

A　7,000 tons

B　7,500 tons

C　75,000 tons

D　750,000 tons

To answer this question you count the number of cotton symbols used for 1860 and then multiply this figure by 1,000 (each symbol represents one thousand tons of cotton).

Pictographs are often used to show population statistics. Typically they use stick figures like this to represent people.

Your next task is to make a pictograph of the U.S. population using information in the table below.

Non-White U.S. Population by Race or Hispanic/Latino Origin, 2000

(🧍 = ten million people)

Race	Population
Hispanic/Latino	3.50
African American	3.00
Asian	1.00
Other	0.75

Arrange the pictograph in the same way as the one on the left. You will need to provide a label for each racial group and to create a symbol to represent people. Be sure to indicate that each symbol represents ten million people.

17 **Use the information in the table above to complete the pictograph below.**

Non-White U.S. Population by Race or Hispanic/Latino Origin, 2000

---

9 Understanding Pictures and Cartoons

Dust storm in Rolla, Kansas in 1935

You can learn a tremendous amount from a picture. It may take pages of writing to provide the information contained in one small photograph. Social studies uses all kinds of pictures to learn what people and places looked like. Important men and women regularly had their portraits painted. Once photography developed during the 1800s, people were more likely to be snapped than painted.

Artists and photographers have captured places as well as people. Early paintings were likely to show country scenes. However, after 1800, attention increasingly turned to factories and cities.

The world's great libraries are storehouses of pictures as well as books. The Library of Congress in Washington has millions of paintings, drawings, prints, photographs, and engravings. When you see an interesting photograph or painting in a text, check the caption to see which institution owns the original.

Charles P. Williams of Kansas sent the photograph above to President Roosevelt. It shows a dust storm approaching the village of Rolla in 1935.

1 **How might Charles Williams have described the storm?**

   A   Darkness came when it hit us.

   B   Every building was burned to the ground

   C   No one survived.

   D   Our houses were washed clean.

Photographs

*Abraham Lincoln in about 1847,
photograph by Nicholas Shepherd*

*Abraham Lincoln in about 1857,
photograph by Alexander Hesler*

*Abraham Lincoln in about 1858,
photograph by Calvin Jackson*

*Abraham Lincoln in about 1860,
photograph by Alexander Hesler*

*Abraham Lincoln in about 1865,
photograph by Alexander Gardner*

On this page you can see five photographs of Abraham Lincoln. The first, on the top left, was taken when Lincoln was a 37-year-old Congressman from the state of Illinois. Moving to the right, the next photo was taken 10 years later around the time of his nomination for the U.S. Senate. The next photo was taken the following year during the Lincoln-Douglas debates on slavery. The photo on the lower left was taken in 1860 about six months before Lincoln was elected President, and the last one was taken at the end of the Civil War, two weeks before his assassination in 1865.

2 **Study the photos carefully. How did a life in politics change Lincoln's appearance?**

_____

_____

_____

_____

_____

A photograph may tell you about people (like President Lincoln), or an event (the Great Dust Storm), or a particular place, or about all three at the same time like the photograph below.

Spreading tar on a London street in 1918, photograph by Horace W. Nicholls

Suppose you were taking a global history test. You might be shown a photograph like the one above and then asked about it. Try answering the following question.

3 **What change in working life does this picture illustrate?**

   A As disease spread and the population grew weaker, basic maintenance work was not getting done.

   B Many men were serving in the armed forces during World War I and women were doing their jobs.

   C New road-building equipment had eliminated the need for human labor.

   D The armed forces were obliged to do much of the work that had previously been done by civilians.

If you had some prior knowledge of English history and noticed the date of the photograph, you would answer this question effortlessly. But even if you did not know that World War I was in progress in 1918, you could still answer correctly by a process of elimination. The photo is an illustration of road maintenance, so Choice A must be

incorrect. It shows three women at work, so machines had not eliminated their jobs and Choice C must be incorrect. None of these women are wearing military uniforms, so Choice D must also be incorrect. This leaves Choice B as the correct answer.

Now find the information you need in the photograph below to answer the next question.

San Francisco after the 1906 earthquake and fire.

4 **You can infer from this photograph that —**

   A. San Francisco made a swift recovery from the devastating earthquake of 1906

   B the center of San Francisco was completely flattened by the earthquake of 1906

   C the fire that followed the 1906 earthquake damaged San Francisco's buildings as much as the earthquake itself

   D the people of San Francisco fled from the city after the 1906 earthquake

Royal Photographic Society

Library of Congress

Paintings

The Virginia House of Burgesses painted by Jack Clifton

So far, all the pictures you have analyzed in this chapter have been photographs. To know what America looked like in colonial times or in the early days of the Republic, we rely on paintings.

The famous painting above shows the Virginia House of Burgesses during the seventeenth century. Study it carefully and decide what it tells you.

5 What do you learn from this painting about self-government in colonial Virginia?

When you answer this, be sure you provide only the information the question asks for. This painting tells you many things. but some of them have nothing to do with the question, for example, the kind of clothes that Virginia's burgesses wore.

Your task is to decide what the painting reveals about the colony's government. One thing you may notice is that all the burgesses were men. You can infer that women did not play any public role in government. The room is fairly small—it seems to contain fewer than forty people. Even if there were no written records of the House of Burgesses, you could use this pictorial record to guess at its size.

This seems to be an orderly gathering, even though no one is obviously in charge. The burgesses listened to the person speaking. They didn't talk among themselves or try to interrupt him. No one is sleeping, or eating, or playing cards. It's true that there are soldiers standing guard around the room. Could they be there to keep order? Or do you think they were protecting the Burgesses against someone else, and if so, whom? Altogether, you might conclude that the meeting is so orderly, that perhaps this is not a portrait from life, but an idealized version of the House of Burgesses.

Cartoons

"That immigration problem again!" —Lute Pease
in the Newark Evening News, 1921

Most cartoons are comments on the political events of the time. Today's cartoons look at the conduct of the government in Washington, at foreign affairs, and at local news. The cartoon shown above was a commentary on an issue that was upsetting many people in 1921.

6 **What issue is the subject of this cartoon?**

A Foreign wars

B Immigration

C Patriotism

D Poverty

To answer this question correctly, you need to look at the different parts of the cartoon. The two figures are symbols. Clearly Uncle Sam represents the U.S. Who does the old woman represent?

You must look at the words it contains to make sense of the drawing:

- U.S. PUBLIC SENTIMENT
- NO DUMPING GROUND FOR REFUSE
- UNDESIRABLES FOR AMERICA
- SOME EUROPEAN OFFICIALS

7 **What or who are the "Undesirables" and "refuse"? What is the viewpoint of the cartoonist on this topic?**

_____

_____

_____

_____

_____

_____

_____

John Adams's study, Adams National Historical Park, Quincy, MA

1   **What can you learn about John Adams, Second President of the United States, from this photograph of his study, the room in which he died in 1826?**

_____

_____

_____

_____

_____

_____

_____

Major Trading Partners of the U.S. for 2000
(all countries listed are in the top 10 for imports and/or exports)

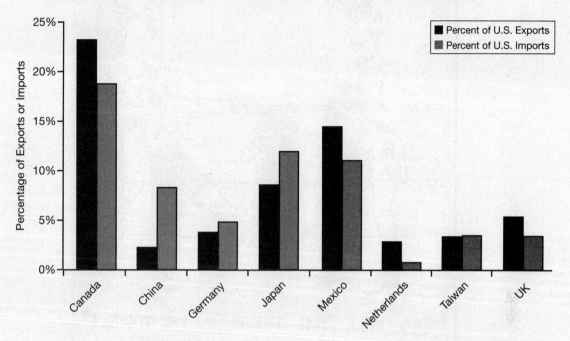

2 After Canada, to which nation does the U.S. export the <u>most</u> goods?

  F Canada

  G China

  H Japan

  J Mexico

3 What percentage of U.S. exports are sent to Canada?

  A About 18 percent

  B About 23 percent

  C About 25 percent

  D About 41 percent

4 Half the information in the bar chart above deals with exports. Use this information to complete the pie chart below. Label each slice of the pie—one slice is already filled in to help you. (No need to use shading.)

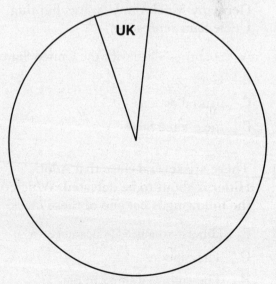

**Nations that Buy
the Most U.S. Exports**

"NOW, WILL YOU THROW IN THE TOWEL!"

Cartoon drawn between 1940 and 1946 by Private Michie Miyamoto, U.S. Army

5 This cartoon was drawn during World War II. It shows Uncle Sam standing and a seated Adolf Hitler, the leader of Germany which the U.S. was fighting. Uncle Sam represents—

A   countries allied with the United States

B   Germany

C   neutral nations

D   the United States

6 There are several clues that Adolf Hitler is about to be defeated. Which of the following is *not* one of these clues?

F   Hitler's exhausted appearance

G   The caption

H   The vulture waiting to pick at Hitler's carcass

J   Uncle Sam's boxing gloves

7 Create a pictograph to show how many hours of TV you watch on the average weekday and on the average weekend day. Create a symbol to represent an hour of TV watching. Provide one label for the average weekday, and one for the average weekend days. Give your graph a title.

V History Skills

This section deals with social studies skills particularly related to the study of history. Understanding the sequence in which events occur is a must for students of history. To help them master this, historians arrange events on graphics known as time lines. The next chapter reviews different time lines and how to use them.

Without a time machine, history can only be viewed through people's thoughts and memories. Even a filmed documentary tells only part of the story—for every moment that made it to the final cut, dozens or hundreds of moments did not, and people had to make those choices. This explains why we include chapters on primary and secondary documents, and on viewpoint and bias. Students must be able to distinguish between primary sources—those created by eyewitnesses or participants in events—and secondary sources, which are second-hand accounts.

One of the toughest tasks that face students of the past (and the present) is detecting **bias**. All authors are biased. They have a point of view that colors their writing. There is nothing wrong with this, but it's important to know that it exists and to understand how it affects what is written. In particular, readers must be able to distinguish between facts and opinions.

It is interesting to compare the viewpoints of two historians writing on the same topic. There's no need to look to the past to find opposing points of view. The Op-Ed pages of today's newspapers are filled with editors expressing their opinions and readers writing in to disagree with them and with each other.

Propaganda is a special kind of bias. It is written (or drawn) with a clear purpose: to persuade people to adopt a particular point of view. In itself, this is no different from a lot of other writing. But propaganda often includes lies and other *intentional* distortions of the truth. It is a tool that governments and political parties use to win over the hearts and minds of the people.

Joseph Goebbels, Minister of Propaganda in Adolf Hitler's Nazi government, alters the words of a poster

Cartoon by Edwin Marcus, 1944; Library of Congress

GLOSSARY

bias: prejudice, tilt, usually against something or someone

1500	1600	1700	1800	1900	2000

| 1492 Columbus sails across the Atlantic—the first crossing in modern times | 1807 Steamboat first used in the U.S.A. | 1825 First railroad (in Britain) | 1880's First cars | 1903 First airplane flight | 1969 First person on moon |

Time lines show the order in which events occurred. Another way of saying this is that they show events in **chronological** sequence.

This time line covers the period from about 1500 to 2000. The first event it shows occurred in 1492, when Columbus sailed across the Atlantic Ocean. The last event is the first moon walk.

Now answer some questions about the time line.

1 In what year did the first moon walk occur?

A   1903

B   1945

C   1969

D   2000

2 About how many years after Columbus's voyage was the first airplane flight?

A   200 years

B   300 years

C   400 years

D   500 years

3 Which type of transportation was used first?

A   Automobiles

B   Sailing ships

C   Steamboats

D   Trains

4 Time lines usually have titles. Which of the following would be the <u>best</u> title for this time line?

A   "Advances in Transportation"

B   "Changes in Communications"

C   "Discoveries in the New World"

D   "The Industrial Revolution"

GLOSSARY

chronological: in time sequence, according to the order in which an event occurred

The events shown in the time line on the opposite page all occurred since year 1 (the year Jesus Christ was born). In time lines since year 1, the years increase towards the right.

In time lines that shows events before year 1, the years increase towards the left. The greater the date, the longer ago an event occurred.

Historians used to label events before year 1 as B.C. (before Christ) and events after year 1 as A.D. (Anno Domini). This Latin term means in the year of our Lord. Nowadays, the years since year 1 are often called the Common Era (C.E.). Events before this are called B.C.E. (before the Common Era).

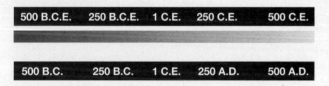

Both styles are shown in the empty time lines above. For the rest of this chapter, we will use the B.C.E./C.E. method.

5 **Which is the earliest date?**

A   1 C.E.

B   270 B.C.E.

C   270 C.E.

D   2700 B.C.E.

Some events occur at a particular date, the Declaration of Independence is an example. Others occur gradually over time and it is hard to pinpoint when they begin and end. Westward expansion in the British colonies, is an example of this. Where a time line does not provide a specific date for an event, you can assume it happened over a period of time.

The time line at the bottom of this page runs from 500 B.C.E. to the present. Look at it carefully and answer the questions.

6 **Which event did *not* begin on any particular date?**

A   Beginning of feudalism

B   Declaration of American independence

C   End of French absolute monarchy

D   End of Roman Republic

7 **What is the modern way to write the first year of the Roman Empire?**

A   27

B   27 A.D.

C   27 C.E.

D   27 B.C.E.

8 **Which event was the first to occur?**

A   The creation of democracy in Athens

B   The beginning of the Roman Empire

C   The end of feudalism

D   The creation of the American Republic

Milestones in the Development of Political Systems

500 B.C.E.	1 C.E.	500 C.E.	1000 C.E.	1500 C.E.	2000 C.E.
509 Athens becomes a democracy	**27** Roman Republic ends, Roman Empire begins		Beginning of feudalism	**1776** American colonies declare independence from Britain and create a republic	**1789** French Revolution ends absolute monarchy

Making Your Own Time Lines

Most time lines deal with major historical events. But a time line can contain any kind of information, provided events are shown in chronological order.

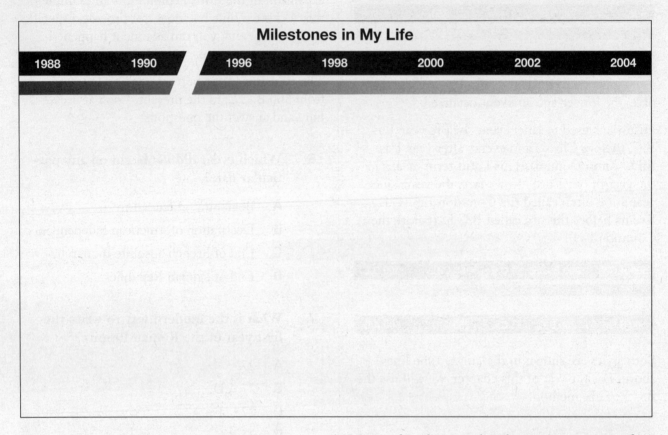

9 Fill in the empty time line above with some major events in your own life. Use the time line on page 108 as a guide. Remember to sort events chronologically. Identify the date of each event and give a short summary of it.

Notice that this time line has a piece cut out of it. Historians do this to show when a number of years has been skipped. In this time line, six years, from 1990 to 1996, are missing. You were a young child then. Hopefully, no major events occurred in your life in these years. If they did, you will have to leave them out.

Now that you have some experience in creating a time line, you can make another one from some major sports events. The table shows the dates of some sports milestones. Sort them out chronologically and enter them into the time line at the bottom of the page. To make these events fit on the time line, you will need to summarize them.

U.S. SPORTING TRIUMPHS

Event	Year
Buccaneers Triumph in Super Bowl	2003
Diver Greg Lougainis wins three Olympic gold medals	1984
Lance Armstrong beats cancer to win Tour De France Cycling Race	1999
Michael Jordan leads Chicago Bulls to win NBA Championship	1985
Serena Williams wins Australian Open, her fourth (tennis) Grand Slam in a row	2003
Tara Lipinski wins Olympic Gold in figure skating	1998
Tiger Woods wins first major golf tournament	1996
Yankees win World Series for the second year in a row	1998

10 Complete the time line below using the events shown in the table above.

Major U.S. Sporting Events of the Past Twenty Years

1984	1986	1988	1990	1992	1994	1996	1998	2000	2002	2004

11 Interpreting Primary and Secondary Sources

Primary Sources

A **primary source** is a *written* record left behind by someone who was an eyewitness to or took part in an event. Primary sources include letters, diaries, autobiographies, property deeds, invoices, even shopping lists. Archeologists who study earlier eras, before records were written, use different kinds of evidence like pottery, bones, jewelry, and ruins.

Here are four examples of different kinds of primary sources:

> Once again, the hopeless cowardly Americans were back to repeat their cowardly act hiding behind a technological advance…The missile attack on Iraq took place around 9 o'clock this morning. This is going to be a glorious day…. the cowardly aggressors will be condemned by both history and the whole world, having been condemned by God Almighty.
>
> Oh, men of our air defenses and our air hawks, from now on consider as non-existent their damned imaginary no-fly zones above 36 parallel and below 32 parallel. Strike with efficiency and competence, in the name of God, any of the aggressors' planes which violate the air space of your great country and everywhere in Iraq, now and in the future.
>
> *Excerpt from Saddam Hussein's speech to the People of Iraq, September 3, 1996*

> I rose at 5 o'clock and wrote a letter to Major Burwell about his boat…I read two chapters in Hebrew and some Greek in Thucydides. I said my prayers and ate boiled milk for breakfast. I danced my dance. I read a sermon in Dr. Tillotson and then took a little [sleep]. I ate fish for dinner.
>
> In the afternoon my wife …read a sermon in Dr. Tillotson to me…I read a little Latin. In the evening we took a walk about the plantation. I neglected to say my prayers but had good health, good thoughts, and good humor, thanks be to God.
>
> This month there were many people sick of fever and pain in their heads; perhaps this might be caused by the cold weather which we had this month, which was indeed the coldest that ever was known in July in this country. Several of my people have been sick, but none died, thank God.
>
> *Diary of William Byrd of Virginia, July 30, 1710*

[Ben] Franklin's character you know. His masterly acquaintance with the French language...his great experience in life, his wisdom, his prudence, caution; his engaging addresses, united to his unshaken firmness in the present American system of war and politics, point him out as the fittest character...[for a mission to Montreal]

John Adams writing to James Warren, 1776

ACCOUNT BOOK OF PETER VAN GAASBEEK
Kingston, N.Y., March 23, 1791

	pounds	shillings	pence
Arthur Copper			
2 pounds of sugar		2	
1/4 pound of tea		1	
1 pepper box			8
1 brush		2	
2 calves' shins	1	5	
1 gin case		1	6
1 pair stockings		5	9
1 pair curtain calico	5	15	
3 yds calico binding			15
1 comb			9
6 plates		15	
1 pound of shot			10

In each of the documents on this and the preceding page, the writer describes his own views, or events in his own life, or his business dealings. Answer these questions about the documents

1 **Saddam Hussein is complaining about —**

A a missile attack on sites in Iraq

B the 1991 Gulf War

C the friendship between the United States and his old enemy, Iran

D the 2003 U.S. invasion of Iraq

2 **What can you learn about Peter Van Gaasbeek from his Account Book?**

A He overcharged his customers.

B He sold a wide variety of items.

C He specialized in fruit and vegetables.

D He was a very wealthy man.

3 **William Byrd —**

A mistreated people

B never took any exercise

C read books in foreign languages

D was very ill

4 **John Adams' probably thought that Ben Franklin —**

A should retire from public life

B should be Prime Minister of Canada

C should be ambassador to France

D was a traitor to his people

5 **Of the men referred to in the documents, which two did *not* know each other?**

A Ben Franklin and John Adams

B John Adams and James Warren

C Peter Van Gaasbeek and Arthur Copper

D William Byrd and Arthur Copper

6 **The passage by Saddam Hussein differs in many ways from the other three documents. Which of the following is *not* one of these ways?**

A It deals with financial matters.

B It was produced in the twentieth century.

C It was produced outside North America.

D It was spoken rather than written.

Secondary Sources

As you have seen, primary sources may come from the distant past as well as from yesterday and today. Historians visit libraries, archives, museums, and records offices where all kinds of primary sources are stored. They also view micro-films of documents and read **digitized** images of text on their computers.

The meaning of primary sources is not always obvious. Historians must interpret them to make sense of them. Their writings are **secondary sources**. In a court of law, the evidence given by people who did not witness an event is called hearsay. All secondary sources are hearsay. They are versions of an event provided by people who did not witness it. Writers of secondary sources rely on the accounts of people who were present, or on other kinds of primary sources like accounts, property deeds, letters, and diaries.

7 **Which of the following is a secondary source?**

A A documentary film about the Altamont Music Festival

B A newspaper account of the trial of a famous mobster written by a journalist who was present at the trial.

C An essay about the Vietnam War written by one of your classmates

D An interview with a woman who worked as a slave on a plantation in South Carolina

The correct answer is the essay written by your classmate. He or she was not present at the war. His or her account is based on the reports of people who were there. All the other choices are eye-witness accounts of events.

GLOSSARY

digitized: converted into numeric form for use by a computer

secondary source: an account by someone not present at the events described

Now read the next four passages and decide which is the secondary source.

A We are unanimously of the opinion that the law passed by the legislature of Maryland, imposing a tax on the Bank of the United States, is unconstitutional and void.

Chief Justice John C. Marshall in the case of McCulloch v. Maryland, *1819*

B We hold these truths to be self-evident, that all men are created equal, that they are endowed by their Creator with certain unalienable Rights, that among these are Life, Liberty and the pursuit of Happiness.

The Declaration of Independence, 1776

C My great-grandmother, Anna Maria...was born in Castlebar, Mayo, sometime between 1845 and 1850...In 1866 or 1867, she and her mother made the eight weeks voyage in a sailing vessel which brought her to New York. Of Ireland she rarely spoke, save to recall that she was often hungry there.

An Irish Integrity by William Alfred

D Mentally, I'm exhausted. I don't feel I have a challenge. Physically, I feel great. " said the 35-year-old Jordan. "This is a perfect time for me to walk away from the game."

Michael Jordan Press Conference, Chicago, Jan. 13, 1999

8 **Which passage above is a secondary source?**

A Passage A

B Passage B

C Passage C

D Passage D

It is interesting to compare primary and secondary accounts of the same events. Both the passages below describe the impact of the Great Depression on the people who lived through it. The first account is taken from a history textbook. The second is an eyewitness account from an out-of-work man in Massachusetts.

> By early 1933...unemployment stood at 25 % or nearly 13 million workers...Men hopped freight trains and rode from city to city, hoping to find work. Others sold pencils or apples to earn a few dollars... Heartrending scenes unfolded as farm families lost their homes...For depression-era children, poor diet and inadequate medical and dental care often led to long-term health problems...The suicide rate climbed nearly 30 % between 1928 and 1932.
>
> *From* The Enduring Vision, A History of the American People, *published in 2000*

> For several minutes I watched an elderly man who stood on a deserted corner near the enormous and idle Everett Mills in the posture of an undotted question mark. He did not see me. Every now and then he swung his arms, not because it was cold, but no doubt because he wanted activity other than walking around, which he probably had been doing for years in a vain effort to get a job. He mumbled to himself...I noticed that his overcoat was split in the back and that his heels were worn off completely.
>
> *Description by Louis Adamic of a jobless man he saw in Lawrence, Massachusetts, during the Great Depression*

9 **What do you learn from the eyewitness account that you do not learn from the textbook?**

_____

_____

_____

10 **Identify one item of information that is in the textbook but not the eyewitness account.**

_____

_____

_____

11 **Write two short passages about cooking. First, in a primary source, describe your own experience of cooking something. Then write a secondary source by a newspaper reporter about cooking done by local students.**

_____

_____

_____

_____

_____

_____

_____

_____

_____

Identifying Viewpoint and Bias

Author's Point of View

Writers, speakers, and artists have their own points of view. Often they would like to persuade you, the viewer or listener, to share their attitudes, and they use many methods to achieve this. In this chapter you will learn some ways of deciding how an author feels about a topic. You will also learn some of the techniques writers use to persuade readers to share their points of view.

Library of Congress

Drawing by Willard Wetmore Combes in about 1940

Take a careful look at the cartoon above and then answer three questions about it.

1 **What exactly does this cartoon show? (Don't try to interpret its meaning yet.)**

_____

_____

_____

_____

2 **What is the message or meaning of the cartoon?**

_____

_____

_____

_____

3 **How does the cartoonist feel about the subject of the drawing?**

_____

_____

_____

_____

_____

A swastika is painted on the boot. This was the symbol of the German Nazi party. If you knew this, you could identify the boot as a Nazi jackboot.

The boot is poised above a city. The message is clear: the Nazis want to crush the world. It's easy to decide that the cartoonist viewed the Nazis as dangerous bullies.

Sometimes a writer will express his or her point of view clearly. When this is not the case, you can often infer where he or she stands from the language the author uses, the examples given, and the way a passage is put together.

Read a passage from *Up From Slavery*, by the black educator, Booker T. Washington.

I cannot remember a single instance during my childhood or early boyhood when our entire family sat down to the table together, and God's blessing was asked, and the family ate a meal in a civilized manner. On the plantation in Virginia, and even later, meals were gotten by the children very much as dumb animals get theirs. It was a piece of bread here and a scrap of meat there. It was a cup of milk at one time and some potatoes at another. Sometimes a portion of our family would eat out of the skillet or pot, while some one else would eat from a tin plate held on the knees, and often using nothing but the hands with which to hold the food.

4 **In you own words, describe how Booker T. Washington felt about the meals he ate as a boy.**

_____

_____

_____

_____

_____

_____

_____

The next passage describes tensions between Native Americans and white settlers in Nevada. Its tone is neutral. Write about this topic from the viewpoints of a white settler and a Paiute Indian.

Early settlers in Paradise Valley faced Indian raids until about 1868, with one particularly severe outbreak in 1865. There is no clear evidence that white settlers displaced the more or less nomadic Northern Paiutes from the valley, but the period was a difficult one for Indian-white relations throughout the state. Thousands of whites entered Nevada after the discovery of silver in 1859, and the inevitable conflicts began...the cavalry fort Camp Winfield Scott was established in 1866.

From the Buckaroos in Paradise Collection, Library of Congress

5 **Describe the Paiute Indians from the viewpoint of a white settler.**

_____

_____

_____

_____

_____

6 **Describe the white settlers from the viewpoint of a Paiute Indian.**

_____

_____

_____

_____

_____

Comparing and Contrasting Points of View

For every strongly held opinion, you may be sure that someone will hold an opposing point of view.

Here is an example of two opposing points of view on the subject of begging on public transportation.

SUBWAY BEGGING, BY PHYLLIS MURPHY

Last Friday I traveled from Newark to mid-town Manhattan by way of the PATH train. During this journey, no fewer than ten pan-handlers passed through my carriage. Each one had a different story, but the message was the same: gimme, gimme, gimme. Why must passengers endure these constant verbal assaults? In fact, some of these beggars can be physically dangerous. One dirty, beefy woman pushed her demanding fist within six inches of my face. The people who run the PATH System complain that subway ridership has gone down. Is it any wonder?

IT COULD BE YOU, BY HUBERT LOPEZ

I was horrified by Phyllis Murphy's lack of compassion (See "Ban Subway Begging" in yesterday's Dispatch.) Does she think people like to spend their days and nights asking strangers for money? They ask for money because they don't have enough to feed, clothe, and house themselves. Society—and that means you and me—has an obligation to its poor. We should count our blessings that we have something to give. One day, that begging hand could be ours. One more thing: the right to beg is protected by the Constitution. It is another form of free speech.

7 **Give one reason used by each writer to support his or her point of view**

_____

_____

Now read two passages showing how prominent politicians disagreed about the 2001 tax cut.

> We put a significant tax relief package in place right at the right time. Our economy was beginning to slow down....And when the econ-omy slows down, it makes sense to cut taxes...I think raising taxes in the midst of a recession is wrong economic policy. It would be a huge mistake, it's bad for American workers ...[and it hurts] when it comes to creating jobs.
>
> _President George W. Bush, January 16, 2002_

> Because Congress [approved] the President's tax-cut request, the federal revenues we will need in order to deal with the current crisis [the terrorism threat that followed 9/11] will not be there. Unless we act, Federal revenues will be more than $100 billion lower than they would have been over the next 10 years because the President persuaded Congress to reduce the tax rate.
>
> _Congressman Barney Frank, Nov. 11, 2001_

8 **Why did President Bush support a tax cut?**

A   He hoped to reduce the national debt.

B   He thought it would boost the economy.

C   He wanted to cut incomes.

D   He wanted to hire more civil servants.

9 **Congressman Frank opposed a tax cut because he thought the government —**

A   had to rev up the economy

B   needed money for homeland security

C   needed to give more help to farmers

D   needed to improve the public schools

Distinguishing Fact from Opinion

When you read a passage, it is important to distinguish between facts and opinions.

Facts can be checked and proven. If a meteorologist claims "five inches of rain fell on Houston yesterday," you can verify this statement.

An opinion is based on the writer's feelings. It cannot be proven the way a fact can. Words like *think*, *feel*, and *believe* indicate that what you are reading is an opinion.

Read the four passages below.

A

> Those bored with foreign countries generally are less likely to study international politics and history.
>
> *Michael J. Totten writing in the*
> Wall Street Journal, *May 12, 2003*

B

> Historically, bison numbered an estimated 20 million to 30 million. Today, approximately 250,000 remain in the United States. Of those only 16,000 roam in the wild. Yellowstone National Park has the only population of free-roaming bison.
>
> *www.kidsplanet.org website*

C

> There is absolutely no chance that Saddam Hussein and his Baathist Party or those who are following Saddam Hussein are ever going to come to power again in Iraq.
>
> *Gen. Richard Myers, Chairman Joint Chiefs of Staff, quoted in* USA Today, *May 12, 2003*

D

> Our waiter and assistant waitress were just fabulous. Since this ship was completely booked, we did have to eat with another family. They were wonderful and friendly and we all had a good time. Then there are those midnight buffets—go to them, they are worth the extra calories.
>
> *Passenger review of Carnival Line cruise,*
> *July 24, 2000*

10 **Which of these passages is *not* an opinion?**

A   Passage A

B   Passage B

C   Passage C

D   Passage D

Three of these passages contain the thoughts and ideas of the individuals who wrote them. Michael Totten tells us what he thinks about people who are bored with foreign countries. General Richard Myers gives his views on the future of Iraq. And a very satisfied customer gives his impression of a cruise aboard a Carnival ship. All three passages are opinions. Only the information on the kidsplanet website is factual. It gives us information about the bison population in the United States.

Now write a passage on the subject of fast food—the kind of food they serve in McDonalds.

11 **Write two sentences about fast food. One sentence should be factual and one should contain your opinion.**

_____

_____

_____

_____

_____

_____

_____

Now read four more passages. This time, three of these passages are filled with facts and one is an opinion. Decide which is which.

A
> Never in the field of human conflict was so much owed by so many to so few.
>
> *Prime Minister Winston Churchill referring to Royal Air Force pilots, August 20, 1940*

B
> On the night of the tenth of May [1940]... I acquired the chief power in the state, which I wielded for five years and three months of world war, at the end of which time, all our enemies having surrendered unconditional-ly...I was immediately dismissed by the British electorate from all further conduct of their affairs.
>
> *Winston Churchill in* The Gathering Storm, *(1947)*

C
> The WPA built or repaired...nearly 600,000 miles of highways, streets, and roads, and laid 24,000 miles of sidewalks. It constructed or restored more than 110,000 public libraries, schools, auditoriums, stadiums, and other public buildings. It constructed 5,898 playgrounds and athletic fields and 1,667 parks, fairgrounds, and rodeo grounds.
>
> *From* The Hungry Years *by T. H. Watkins*

D
> Millions of people have moved from rural areas into [India's] cities. On the farm, a husband and wife must count on their many children for help in the fields and for support in old age. In the city things are different. There a worker can get a pension upon retirement.
>
> *From* Global Geography *by Finkelstein, Flanagan, and Lunger*

12 **Which of these passages is an opinion?**

A Passage A

B Passage B

C Passage C

D Passage D

13 **For each of the passages, explain in one sentence why you decided that the passage contained facts or opinions.**

_____

_____

_____

_____

_____

_____

_____

_____

_____

_____

_____

Propaganda

In the name of God, the most gracious, the Most Merciful; oh, great people; oh, honorable members of our armed forces; oh, sons of our glorious Arab nation; oh, honorable people of the world:

Once again, the hopeless cowardly Americans were back to repeat their cowardly act hiding behind a technological advance that God, most gracious, wanted it to be their curse and cause for shame.

The aggressors came back launching their failed cowardly raids to commit a damned third attack which has very significant implications. The courageous resistance and great steadfastness of the noble Iraqi people gave the aggressors what they deserved. They will be taught a lesson and their wanton attack will be resisted.

The missile attack on Iraq took place around 9 o'clock this morning, 3rd of September 1996, corresponding to 20th Rabi' Athani 1417 Hijri. This is going to be a glorious day. The Iraqi people will, in the name of God, add to their honorable record. It will be a day when the cowardly aggressors will be condemned by both history and the whole world, having been condemned by God Almighty.

Oh, Iraqi people and members of the brave Iraqi armed forces, the apple of our eye, this is another day you can call your own. So, resist them as you have done. God Almighty wishes you to take your pride of place under the sun and on the heights of your good land.

We have come to expect you — and your people and the Arab nation are calling upon you — to resist them and teach them a new lesson full of meanings their weak and empty souls do not know.

Oh, men of our air defenses and our air hawks, from now on consider as non-existent their damned imaginary no-fly zones above 36 parallel and below 32 parallel. Strike with efficiency and competence, in the name of God, any of the aggressors' planes which violate the air space of your great country and everywhere in Iraq, now and in the future.

The free peoples of the world and the sons of our glorious Arab nation can rest assured that proud, glorious and defiant Iraq is safe. Iraq is as powerful as high mountains. It will not be shaken by the winds of evil; neither will it be frightened, God willing, by the hiss of vipers.

The sons of the Land of Two Rivers were more than a match to the enemy; they downed a large number of its missiles.

God foiled the aggression and the aggressors and, thanks be to God, we only suffered light losses in the failed attack.

May God bless the souls of our honorable martyrs. God is greater, God is greater. May the cowards be defeated.

Saddam Hussein's speech to the People of Iraq, September 3, 1996

Propaganda takes many forms. It may be found in a lengthy newspaper editorial, in a political leaflet, or even in a school history text.

Propaganda is defined by the dictionary as:

> The use of facts, ideas, or claims to persuade people to support a particular opinion or course of action.

Propaganda uses only those facts or opinions that support the writer's point of view. It is intended to provoke strong feelings. It uses powerful, emotional language that often appeals to religious, national, or ethnic pride (or bias).

You have already read a shorter version of the speech above. This uncut version is an excellent example of propaganda. The speaker abuses his opponents and tries to persuade the Iraqi people to share his bitter anger. Most every paragraph calls on the name of God.

Here is another piece of propaganda, written by another dictator, Adolf Hitler. Look for similarities between Hitler's and Hussein's speeches.

> **APRIL 6, 1941, Order of the Day to the German Army of the East from Fuhrer Adolf Hitler**
>
> Soldiers of the Southeast Front:
>
> Since early this morning the German people are at war with the Belgrade Government of intrigue. We shall only lay down arms when this band of ruffians has been definitely and most emphatically eliminated, and the last Briton has left this part of the European Continent. These misled people realize that they must thank Britain for this situation, they must thank England, the greatest war-monger of all time.
>
> Soldiers of the Southeast Front: Now your zero hour has arrived. You will now take the interests of the German Reich under your protection...In doing this, your duty, you will not be less courageous than the men of those German divisions who in 1915, on the same Balkan soil, fought so victoriously.
>
> We pray to God that He may lead our soldiers on the path and bless them as hitherto....

14 **The speeches by Saddam Hussein and Adolf Hitler have many points in common. How do they differ?**

A Only one of them deals with a ground war.

B Only one of them describes the heroic actions of the nation's troops, past or present.

C Only one of them expects God to lead them to victory.

D Only one of them uses abusive language about their opponents.

Dictators are not the only people who use propaganda. The next passage was created by the U.S. Defense Department. It was broadcast into Afghanistan, ruled then by the Taliban, shortly after the September 11, 2001 attacks. The Taliban had allowed Osama bin Laden and Al Qaeda to set up training camps in Afghanistan. The broadcast occurred before U.S. troops invaded Afghanistan.

> Attention Taliban! You are condemned. Did you know that? The instant the terrorists you support took over our planes, you sentenced yourselves to death. The Armed Forces of the United States are here to seek justice for our dead. Highly trained soldiers are coming to shut down once and for all Osama bin Laden's ring of terrorism, and the Taliban that supports them and their actions.
>
> Our forces are armed with state of the art military equipment. What are you using, obsolete and ineffective weaponry? Our helicopters will rain fire down upon your camps before you detect them on your radar. Our bombs are so accurate we can drop them right through your windows. ...You have only one choice... Surrender now and we will give you a second chance. We will let you live. If you surrender no harm will come to you...Doing this is your only chance of survival.

Remember that propaganda is the use of facts, ideas, or claims to persuade people to support a particular opinion or course of action. Ask yourself what makes this broadcast a piece of propaganda.

15 **Which of the following portions of the broadcast is based on facts rather than opinions?**

A Our forces are armed with state of the art military equipment.

B The instant the terrorists you support took over our planes, you sentenced yourselves to death.

C You are condemned. Did you know that?

D You have only one choice..Surrender now...this is your only chance of survival.

Governments don't have a monopoly on propaganda. It is widely used by industry, by special interest groups, even by charitable foundations. Advertising, product placements, and even fundraising– this kind of propaganda influences people without making its purpose obvious.

For example, clothing manufacturers pay movie stars or pop musicians to wear their garments in everyday life. Fans who idolize the stars want to dress like them. Advertisements that stress the educational benefits and travel opportunities of using their product also use this technique. Propaganda influences what we buy, what we believe, how we behave, and how we make important decisions.

When it comes to sending persuasive messages, pictures can be even more effective than words. These two posters were produced during the world wars. The one below was created by the German government during World War I. The poster intends to encourage citizens to lend money for the war effort (The caption translates this message into English.) The poster on the right was used by the U.S. government during World War II. It aims to persuade citizens to enlist in the army. Compare the two posters and then write about them.

And **your** duty?
Sign the war loan

16 Both posters hope to persuade citizens to take action, but they appeal to different emotions. Explain these differences.

_____

_____

_____

_____

_____

_____

_____

Analyzing Editorials

Newspaper editorials and Letters to the Editor are usually written to persuade readers to take some action or to convince them that the writer is correct. The best way to analyze this kind of writing is to decide on the author's main point, to see how he or she supports this point, and decide which statements are facts and which are opinions.

Suppose you read the following letter:

> Dear Editor,
>
> Today your newspaper showed close-up pictures of Siberian tigers in our local zoo. Patrons of the zoo can now stand just inches from the tigers' faces, separated only by a sheet of glass.
>
> This is all well and good for the families who like to stand and stare at the big cats. But what about the big cats who have to spend their mornings being gaped at by nosy humans? No one asked how they felt about it!
>
> Nowadays, most zoos try to mimic an animal's natural environment so far as possible. The Siberian plains do not include men, women, and children standing in gawking rows.
>
> No doubt the zoo authorities hope to attract more fee-paying customers by offering them a peepshow. But I urge animal lovers everywhere to boycott the zoo until its tigers are given the privacy they deserve.

17   **What is the letter writer's main point?**

_____

_____

_____

_____

_____

18   **What arguments does the writer use to support this point?**

_____

_____

_____

_____

_____

19   **Identify one fact and one opinion in this letter.**

_____

_____

_____

_____

20   **Write a reply to this letter from a different point of view. Be sure to include a main idea and supporting arguments.**

Dear Editor,

_____

_____

_____

_____

_____

_____

_____

_____

A Buddhist monastery known as KTD is perched on top of the mountain that overlooks the small town of Woodstock, New York. A world-famous youth known as the Karmapa heads the Buddhist organization that KTD belongs to. The organization has made Woodstock its North American headquarters. This has led KTD to propose a massive building expansion. Local residents are deeply divided on the issue. Supporters and opponents of the project have showered the local newspaper with their letters.

You can read below excerpts from four of these letters. One is a very emotional response, the other three offer more rational arguments, one for and two against the proposed expansion.

A   I would like to question the future of having a huge temple over our heads on the mountain. A religion, foreign to our country, found the unique free-spirited town of Woodstock and they were proudly welcomed. But [now the town is filled with Buddhists]...decked in gold and blood-red, wanting more, more, and still more. If they do not succeed in satisfying their greed they will fight and one day there will be a Holy War. As with all religions, they believe "THEIRS" is the only right one in the world.

B   How is it possible for the number of bathrooms to increase from 10 to 48 without there being any increase in water usage? How is it possible that the largest commercial kitchen in the area will not produce an increase in water usage?...If Meads Mountain Road and/or McDaniel Road, both narrow, winding roads, must carry increased traffic in the form of supply trucks, buses, and private cars...is [KTD] willing to pay for reconstructing and widening these roads.

C   KTD states "attendance at occasional large ceremonial events will be limited to 1,000... [But] articles on the "Karmapa News" website... estimated that 250,000 people attended [a major Karmapa talk] in 2002 and that 500,000 attended it in 2003.

D   What about the throngs of people who attend the Woodstock Film and Poetry Festivals? Those two events are held right in town and really do screw up traffic, whereas those going to the KTD monastery will be out of town for the most part. To be sure, roadway improvements are needed, but such improvements have been needed for some time... [Opponents say] KTD expansion will create water and sewage problems ... [But] the expanded monastery will reuse its gray water. In so doing, KTD folks show themselves to be friends of the environment and good neighbors.

21   **Which passage uses emotional arguments?**

    A   Passage A

    B   Passage B

    C   Passage C

    D   Passage D

22   **Which passage supports KTD expansion?**

    A   Passage A

    B   Passage B

    C   Passage C

    D   Passage D

23   **Which of the following is one of the _rational_ arguments used against the proposed expansion?**

    A   Other local events create much more serious traffic problems for the town.

    B   Religion always leads to wars.

    C   The access roads to the monastery will have to be widened at town expense.

    D   The KTD monastery will recycle its gray water.

Unit Review

1480	1500	1520	1540	1560	1580	1600

1492
Columbus reaches Caribbean

1494
Treaty of Tordesillas

1497
Cabot reaches Newfoundland

1521
Cortes defeats Aztecs

1534
Cartier travels down St. Lawrence River

1540–1542
Coronado's expedition through Texas to the Grand Canyon

1565
Spanish build forts in Florida

1585
English colony at Roanoke

1588
Defeat of Spanish Armada

1608
Champlain creates French colony at Quebec

1609
Hudson sails up Hudson River

1 In which year did the Spanish build a fort at St. Augustine, their first fort in Florida?

A   1494   C   1540
B   1521   D   1565

2 When did the English establish their first colony in North America?

F   1497 B.C.E.
G   1497 C.E.
H   1585 B.C.E.
J   1585 C.E.

3 How long after the French first explored the St. Lawrence River was the first French colony in Canada created at Quebec?

A   Less than 50 years
B   74 years
C   About 100 years
D   116 years

4 What would be an appropriate title for this time line?

_____

5 Decide which two of the following events belong in the time line above and draw them in.

1488   Díaz reaches southern Africa

1543   De Soto explores Texas

1607   English settle at Jamestown

1648   End of Europe's Thirty Years' War

1672   Joliet and Marquette reach upper Mississippi River

The following letter was written by Captain Archibald Butt, military aide to President Theodore Roosevelt.

July 25, 1908

My dear Mother:

The greatest surprise to me so far has been the utmost simplicity of life at Sagamore Hill. I am constantly asking myself if this can really be the home of the President of the United States, and how is it possible for him to enforce such simplicity in his environment. It might be the home of a well-to-do farmer with literary tastes or the house of some college professor.

There was no one at the house when we got there. Mrs. Roosevelt had been out to see some sick neighbor and the President was playing tennis. They both came in together, however, he in tennis garb and she in a simple white muslin with a large white hat...He welcomed us with his characteristic handshake and she most graciously and kindly. The President was so keen for us to take a swim that he did not give us time to see our rooms before we were on the way to the beach.

I do not know when I have enjoyed anything so much. I could not help remarking how pretty and young Mrs R. looked in her bathing suit. I did not admire his, however, for it was one of those one-piece garments and looked more like a suit of overalls than a bathing suit, and I presume he did not think it dignified for the President to wear one of those abbreviated armless suits which we all think are so becoming...

Dinner was at 8:00 and we hurried home to put on evening clothes....He put Mrs. Winthrop on his right and I sat on his left. There was no special formality, and the only deference which was paid to the President was the fact that all dishes were handed to him first, then to Mrs. Roosevelt, and after that to the guest of honor. Miss Ethel was late in coming to dinner and everyone, including the President, rose. From the conversation which followed I learned that it had always been the rule to be on time for their meals and the President said that he thought that Ethel ought to try to be on time, too...Ethel said that she would try to be on time to all her meals except breakfast.

6 **What would you guess is a major difference between Sagamore Hill and the present-day White House?**

   F Meals were served at Sagamore Hill where family and guests ate together.

   G Sagamore Hill had rooms where visitors could stay.

   H The lack of security at Sagamore Hill

   J The presence of sports facilities at the White House.

7 **Capt. Butt describes the *simplicity* of life at Sagamore Hill. It could also be described as—**

   A fashionable   **C** luxurious

   B informal   **D** undignified

8 **What makes the passage above a primary source?**

   F It was written by someone who learned about life at Sagamore Hill from a friend.

   G It was written by someone who was present at and took part in the events he describes.

   H The author was a historian.

   J This letter was lost and later unearthed by an archeologist digging in the ground near Sagamore Hill.

The two letters to the Editor that follow are reprinted from the *Minneapolis Star Tribune*. They were written in response to a demonstration that occurred during a performance of the Shriner's Circus on July 6, 2003.

NASTY SHRINERS

Last Sunday, a group of animal activists, myself included, protested the Shriner Circus' exploitation of animals used as entertainment.

I am only 18 and I still have respect for those older than me, and expect a certain behavior in return. I was shocked to see Shriners and their wives exhibit such disgusting and rude behavior.

Besides the regular "Get a life" comments, these dignified men and women swore repeatedly, directed often at the young children who were passing out leaflets.

I heard one man ask what the world has come to. I'm asking that as well. I have lost any respect I had for these distinguished Shriners, and perhaps in the future they can stand by their mission statement and be the men of good character they claim to be.

Kathryn Pelka, Edina

ROTTEN WELCOME

I owe my life to the Shriners. In 1969 they provided necessary medical treatment that would have devastated my family financially. They are a very giving organization, providing holiday parties and picnics to all those children they have helped.

To malign them over a circus that they don't own is a discredit to all the care they have provided for children for so many years.

I am ashamed to be a Minnesotan when I see how these fine people have been greeted in our city.

Charles Brose, Coon Rapids.

9 What is Kathryn Pelka's main complaint about the Shriner Circus?

_____

_____

_____

_____

10 What argument does Charles Brose use to defend the Shriners?

_____

_____

_____

11 Charles Brose's letter is a reply to Kathryn Pelka. How might she in turn respond to the arguments that he makes? Write a reply of two sentences.

_____

_____

_____

_____

_____

VI Geography Skills

Geographers divide their subject into five themes: location, place, region, the interaction between people and the environment, and movement. The themes that most interest us in this book are location, place, and region. Where is a place? What is it like? What are the characteristics of a region? These questions can be answered by examining maps.

Maps tell you about the physical world: its oceans and mountains and deserts. They allow you to distinguish between the vegetation or climate or elevation levels of different regions. They show the boundaries that separate one nation or one province from another. Maps also have very practical uses. Road maps tell you how to get to your destination.

Before you can use a map effectively you must learn how to map read. The first chapter in this section describes map keys and scales. You will learn how to use latitude and longitude to find a particular location.

You will learn more about the content of geography in this section than you will about that any of the other social sciences. This is because so much of geography is told in maps. One specialized use of maps is to show how people have changed the natural landscape. Maps (and graphs) are also used to show population statistics—which areas are the most densely populated, and whether or not a population is growing in size.

Map Projections

Our planet Earth is shaped like a ball. The best way to show what it looks like is to use a globe because it, too, is shaped like a ball. As you turn a globe you can see earth's oceans and land masses. Unfortunately, globes are bulky and inconvenient to store and carry. They cannot show areas in any detail. So geographers have created flat maps of the world.

The most accurate way to make a flat map would be to peel off the surface of a globe. If you cut it to flatten it, it would look something like this:

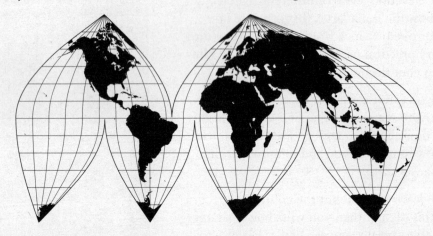

You have created what is known as a map **projection**. Projections are different ways of representing the shape and size of the Earth on a flat surface. For obvious reasons, this one is called a broken projection. Land masses are shaded black and the oceans are white. The problem with this kind of projection is that, while land masses are shown correctly (apart from Antarctica) the oceans are broken into pieces.

1 **What is a map projection?**

    A A globe that shows the planet Earth

    B A way of cutting the surface of the globe to make it fit on a flat surface

    C A way of showing Earth's land masses and oceans on a flat map

    D An exact way of showing the shape and size of oceans and continents

GLOSSARY

projection: representation of the appearance of the Earth on a flat surface

The Mercator projection avoids the problem of cutting the Earth into sections. As you can see, it shows the world's lands and oceans, unbroken, on a flat map. Mercator is accurate for the areas across the center of the Earth. But the land and oceans at the top and bottom of the map are very distorted. They appear much larger than they really are. The continent of Antarctica at the bottom of the map looks almost as large as all the rest of the world. In fact it is only about one tenth the size.

To reduce these distortions, geographers created the Robinson projection which you can see below. Compare these two projections and the broken projection shown opposite and answer the questions.

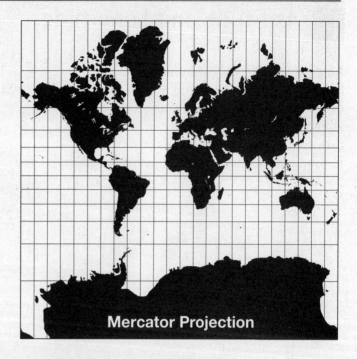

Mercator Projection

Robinson Projection

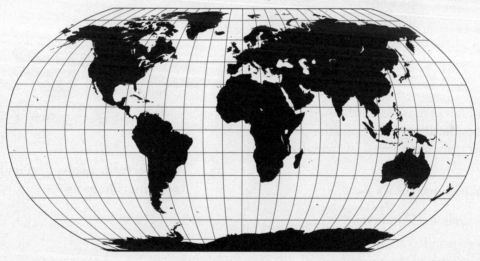

2 **Unlike the Mercator projection, the Robinson projection —**

A distorts the shape and size of Antarctica

B shows how large the Earth is

C shows that Greenland, the large island at the top of the map, is, in fact, much smaller than South America

D shows that less than half the surface of the Earth is covered by water

3 **The broken projection is far more accurate than the Robinson projection and the Mercator projection at showing —**

A how the oceans may be divided into sections

B that Antarctica has a pointed shape

C the correct size and shape of all the Earth's land masses except Antarctica

D the correct size and shape of the middle areas of the Earth

Latitude and Longitude

Lines of latitude and longitude are imaginary bands that run east-west and north-south around the globe. **Lines of latitude** (also known as **parallels**) go east-west. The equator is the parallel that runs around the center of the Earth. Latitudes to the north of the equator are labeled "N" and those to the south are labeled "S."

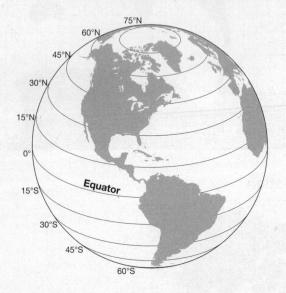

There are 180 lines of latitude. Each one could be shown on a map, but this would make the map very busy. Most maps show just a few parallels.

4 **The map above shows —**

   A parallels at 15° intervals

   B more parallels south of the equator than north of the equator

   C only the parallels south of the equator

   D that the correct way to write a line of latitude below the equator is 10°N

Lines of longitude are also known as **meridians**. They run from the North Pole to the South Pole.

The central line of longitude is called the **Prime Meridian**. On the globe below it is labeled 0°.

Meridians west of the Prime Meridian are labeled "W" and those to its east are labeled "E." If you measure 180° west from the Prime Meridian, you reach the International Date Line (it runs north-south to the west of Alaska). Measure 180° west from there and you have circled the world and reached the Prime Meridian again.

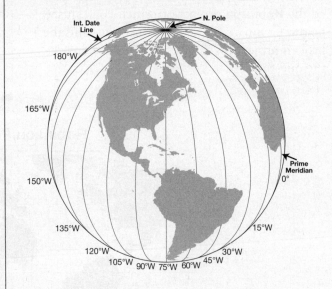

5 **The Mercator projection inaccurately shows meridians as —**

   A curving lines

   B horizontal lines

   C converging lines

   D parallel lines

The lines of latitude are parallel bands around the globe, an equal distance apart. By contrast, all the meridians meet at the poles. This is why the Mercator projection has to be inaccurate—and why the distortion gets worse as you approach the poles.

GLOSSARY

lines of latitude (or parallels): imaginary, east-west lines circling the Earth

lines of longitude (or meridians): imaginary, north-south lines running between the poles and circling the Earth

Prime Meridian: the line of longitude at 0° that runs through Greenwich, England

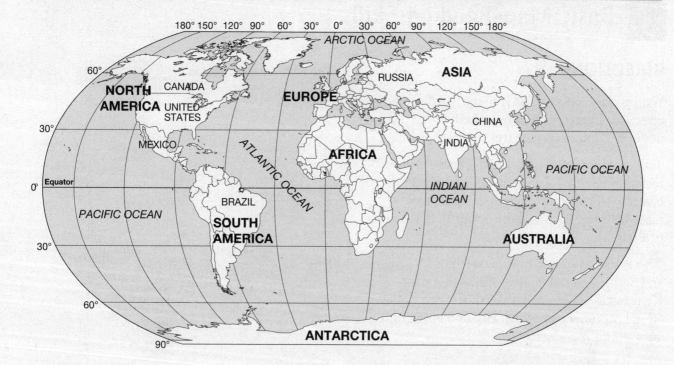

Like the map on page 131, the map above uses the Robinson projection. This map identifies the world's oceans and continents, and its largest countries.

Parallels of latitude and meridians of longitude are used as a means of locating places on a map. Bearing in mind that latitudes are labeled "°N" and "°S" while longitudes are labeled "°E" and "°W," answer the questions that follow.

6 Which of the following is a line of longitude that cuts through the Indian Ocean?

A   60°E

B   60°S

C   120°W

D   The equator

7 Which continent lies at the point where 120°E and 30°S cross each other?

A   Africa

B   Asia

C   Australia

D   South America

8 Which continent lies completely to the north of the equator?

A   Africa

B   Australia

C   North America

D   South America

9 Which of the following continents does the Prime Meridian *not* pass through?

A   Africa

B   Antarctica

C   Asia

D   Europe

10 Which of the following is a location in China?

A   90°E and 30°N

B   90°W and 30°S

C   60°E and 60°N

D   180°E and 60°N

Basic Map-Reading Skills

DIRECTION

You cannot read a map if you don't understand direction. Direction tells you whether one place lies north, south, east, or west of another place.

Take any location in the world—Paris, France, for example. Any place that lies between Paris and the North Pole is north of Paris; any place between Paris and the South Pole is south of Paris.

The Prime Meridian runs between the North and South Poles. The map shows that the Kenyan city of Mombasa lies to the east of the Prime Meridian. The Mali city of Timbuktu is west of this meridian.

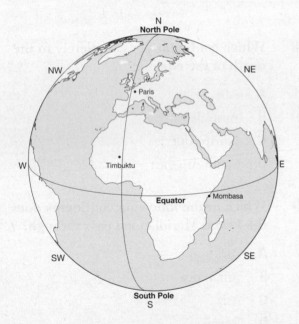

Most maps have a compass to tell you the direction of north, south, east, and west. It may also be useful to know the direction of northeast, southeast, northwest, and southwest. These directions are shown in the globe above.

Study the map at the upper right and answer questions about direction.

The Mid-Atlantic States

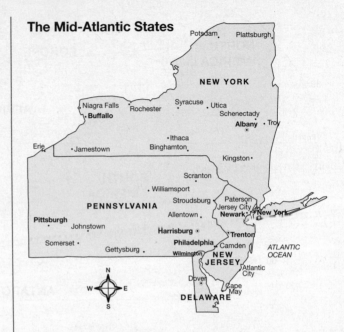

11 The map shows four states. Which state lies furthest to the south?

A   Delaware

B   New Jersey

C   New York

D   Pennsylvania

12 If you traveled from New York City to Pittsburgh, Pennsylvania, you would travel —

A   east

B   north

C   south

D   west

13 Which city lies northeast of Harrisburg?

A   Buffalo

B   Dover

C   Gettysburg

D   Newark

134 | *Social Studies Skillsbook, Intermediate*

MAP SCALE

Even the largest and most detailed maps cannot show an area at its true size. They need to show areas as much, much smaller than they really are. A scale tells you how map size corresponds to true size.

Map distances are usually shown in miles or kilometers. One mile equals 1.6 kilometers (km), so an inch on a map might represent one mile or 1.6 kilometers. A map may tell you:

> one inch represents 100 miles

More likely, a map scale will show you the scale and you must measure it for yourself. The map of Mexico below contains this scale:

```
        200 km
  ├───────────────┤
  0       200 Miles
```

The line below 200 kilometers measures about 3/8ths of an inch and the line above 200 miles measures a little over half an inch—in other words, an inch on the map represents about 400 miles. Use a ruler to measure the distance from the northwest tip of Mexico to the southeast tip. It's about five and 3/8 inches. If one inch is 400 miles, five and 3/8 inches are 2,150 miles.

14 The distance between the most westerly point in Mexico and the most easterly point is about —

A 50 miles

B 2,000 miles

C 5,500 miles

D 20,000 miles

Baja California Norte includes the westernmost point in Mexico and Quintana Roo contains the easternmost point. The distance between these points is about five inches, or 2,000 miles. Now answer another question about scale.

15 Find the point where the states of Chihuahua, Durango, and Coahuila intersect. What is the shortest distance between this point and the Gulf of Mexico?

A About 200 miles

B About 400 miles

C About 800 miles

D About 1,000 miles

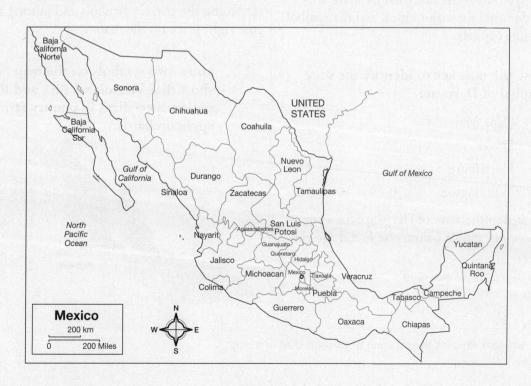

MAP KEYS

Most maps have keys (they are also called **legends**). These keys tell you what the symbols used in the map stand for. Different kinds of maps use different kinds of symbols. Political maps may contain symbols for capital cities. Here is an example:

The Mid-Atlantic States

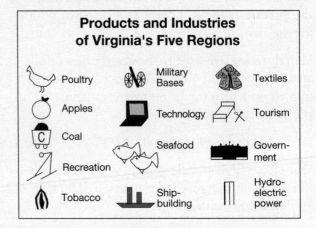

The map key at the upper left of the map identifies three symbols— the line used for state borders, the dot used for major cities, and the symbol used for state capitals.

16 **Use the map key to identify the state capital of Delaware.**

A Cape May

B Dover

C Harrisburg

D Wilmington

If you looked in the state of Delaware for a city with the symbol shown below, you found the correct answer.

⊙ State capital

Most political maps contain only a few symbols and the ones they contain are fairly simple. Maps that show the economy of a particular region may use more complicated symbols.

Products and Industries of Virginia's Five Regions

Poultry · Apples · Coal · Recreation · Tobacco · Military Bases · Technology · Seafood · Ship-building · Textiles · Tourism · Government · Hydro-electric power

Here you can see the key used on a Virginia map. Some symbols represent industries like textiles and ship building. Some show the different animals and crops raised and grown by local farmers. Some show large local employers such as the government. Others show areas popular with vacationers.

Below you can see an outline map of Virginia's five regions. Your task is to draw two symbols on the map. Your artistic skill is less important than choosing the correct symbols and putting them in the right place on the map.

17 **Draw two symbols on the map below to show that Virginia's Valley and Ridge region specializes in poultry farms and apple orchards.**

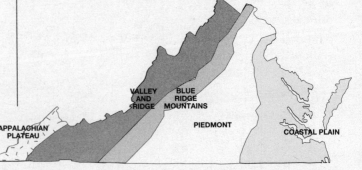

GLOSSARY

legend: key that explains the meaning of symbols used in a map

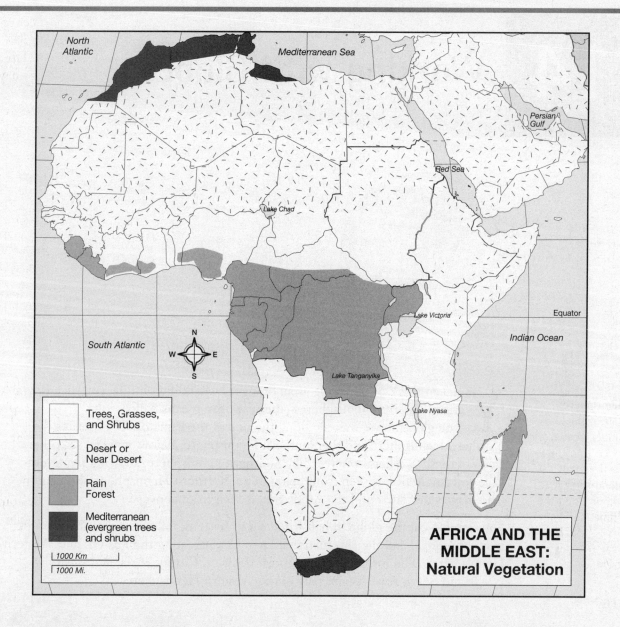

AFRICA AND THE MIDDLE EAST: Natural Vegetation

Map key:
- Trees, Grasses, and Shrubs
- Desert or Near Desert
- Rain Forest
- Mediterranean (evergreen trees and shrubs)

1000 Km
1000 Mi.

Some maps use different shading patterns to show climate zones, or vegetation regions, or religious groups. The map key tells you what these different patterns represent. This map of Africa and the Middle East identifies four kinds of vegetation regions. Use it to answer the questions.

18 **What kind of vegetation would you find in the southern tip of Africa?**

A   Desert

B   Evergreen trees and shrubs

C   Grasses

D   Rain forest

19 **Where in Africa or the Middle East would you find tropical rain forest?**

A   In the coastal areas by the Mediterranean Sea

B   In the lands along the Persian Gulf

C   In the region around the Equator

D   On the east coast of Africa, particularly around Lake Nyasa

GLOSSARY

hemisphere:
half of the
globe, created
by cutting the
Earth in half
along the equa-
tor, or along the
Prime Meridian

You can think of the globe as an orange. Depending on how you slice it, you create different hemispheres—**hemisphere** means half a globe.

The globe above was cut along the line of the Equator. This creates the Northern Hemisphere and the Southern Hemisphere. Below, you can see other views of these two hemispheres. The Southern Hemisphere, showing the South Pole and Antarctica, is seen from below. The Northern Hemisphere, showing the land masses that surround the Arctic Sea, is seen from above.

You can also cut the globe in half from top to bottom, following the curves of the Prime Meridian and the International Date Line, creating the Eastern and Western Hemispheres. The former includes most of Africa, Europe, Asia, and Australia. North and South America are part of the Western Hemisphere.

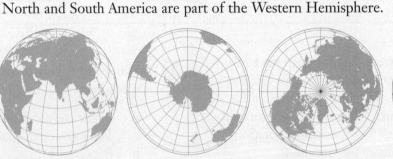

Eastern Hemisphere   **Southern Hemisphere**   **Northern Hemisphere**   **Western Hemisphere**

1   **Each location on planet Earth is in —**

A   only one hemisphere

B   two hemispheres

C   three hemispheres

D   all four hemispheres

Latitudes and Climate

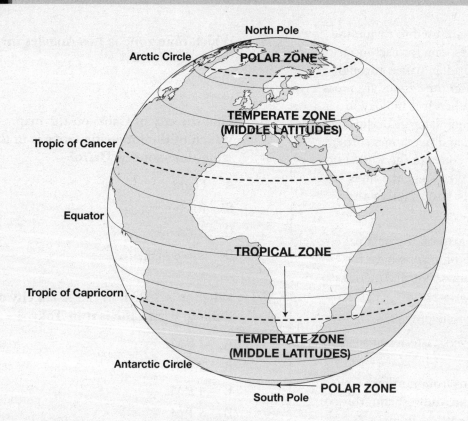

This globe shows how the parallels of latitude divide the world into climate regions. The latitudes near the equator—between the **Tropic of Cancer** and the **Tropic of Capricorn**—are very hot. Their climate is tropical. The latitudes north of the Arctic Circle (around the North Pole) and south of the Antarctic Circle (around the South Pole) are very cold. These regions have a polar climate.

Asia's tropical regions are heavily populated, but most of the rest of the world's people live in the middle latitudes where the climate is fairly mild.

GLOSSARY

Tropic of Cancer: a parallel of latitude north of the equator that forms the northern boundary of the torrid or tropical zone

Tropic of Capricorn: a parallel of latitude south of the equator that forms the southern boundary of the torrid or tropical zone

This view of the globe makes the southern temperate and polar zones appear smaller than those in the north. In fact they are the same size, and this impression is caused by the angle of the globe.

2 **How would you expect the climate in the northern middle latitudes to compare with the climate in the southern middle latitudes?**

A The middle latitudes are warmer in the north.

B The middle latitudes are warmer in the south.

C The middle latitudes in the north and south have the same climate.

D The northern and southern middle latitudes are warmer in the Western Hemisphere and cooler in the Eastern Hemisphere.

Longitude and Time Zones

Meridians of longitude are used to divide the world into 24 time zones, one for each hour of the day. The Prime Meridian passes through Greenwich, England, and time zones are measured from this point. When it is midday in Greenwich, it is two hours later in Berlin, two times zones to the east, and five hours earlier in New York, five time zones to the west. For political or geographical reasons, the lines separating time zones do not always follow the meridians exactly.

Look at the time zone map on the next page. Areas lying in the same time zone have the same shading. For example, North America is divided into six time zones:

- the Canadian maritime provinces;
- Eastern, which covers eastern Canada and the Eastern states;
- Central, which runs from northern Canada through most of the Midwest and Mexico;
- Mountain, which follows the Rocky Mountains, north-south;
- Pacific, covering the west coast areas of Canada, Mexico, and the U.S.; and
- Alaska.

The north-south lines separating these time zones are fairly straight.

3 Which time zone is Los Angeles in?

_____

4 Find the city of Cairo on the map. Which of the following cities is in the same time zone as Cairo?

A   Delhi

B   Johannesburg

C   Moscow

D   Rio de Janeiro

5 When it is 3 P.M. in the Asian city of Beijing, what time is it in Tokyo?

A   2 P.M.

B   3 P.M.

C   4 P.M.

D   5 P.M.

6 In which city is it 12 noon when it is 10 P.M. in Sydney?

A   London

B   Moscow

C   New York City

D   Tokyo

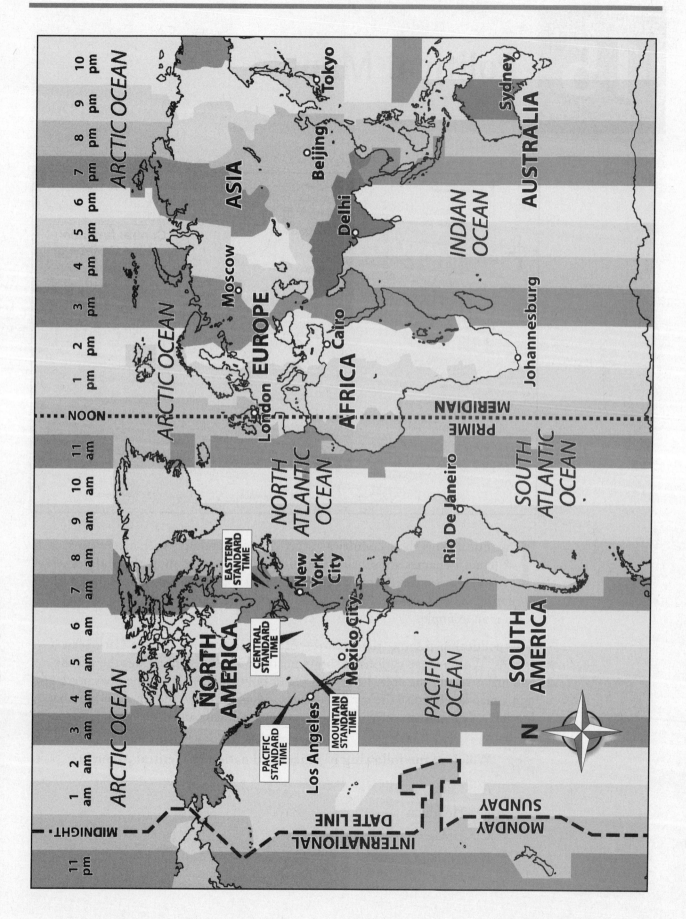

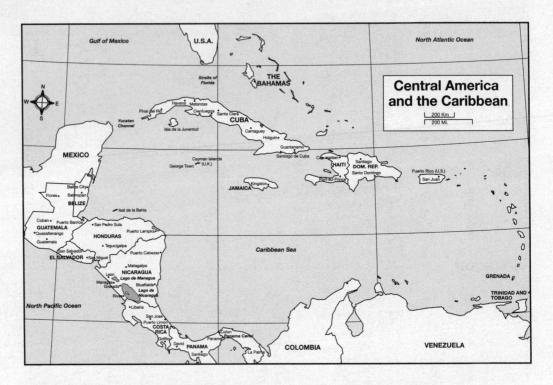

P olitical maps show countries, or provinces or counties within countries (country names are usually capitalized). These maps show the outlines of land masses (like Africa). They identify major bodies of water within or bordering on land masses. And they show cities and towns within land masses. Here is an example:

This political map shows the countries of Central America and the Caribbean Islands. Within these nations, it shows major cities. It also identifies the oceans and major seas in the area. Like some other political maps, this one does not contain a map key because the symbols it uses—dots for cities and lines for national borders—explain themselves. It does contain a compass and a scale.

1 **Which of the following is a mainland nation of Central America?**

    A Cuba

    B Honduras

    C Jamaica

    D Trinidad

The Lands of the Eastern Hemisphere

Political maps of the world, or large parts of it, help you to identify the shapes of the continents and the major countries. The map below shows four of the continents that lie mainly in the Eastern Hemisphere. Notice the dotted lines that show the boundaries between continents.

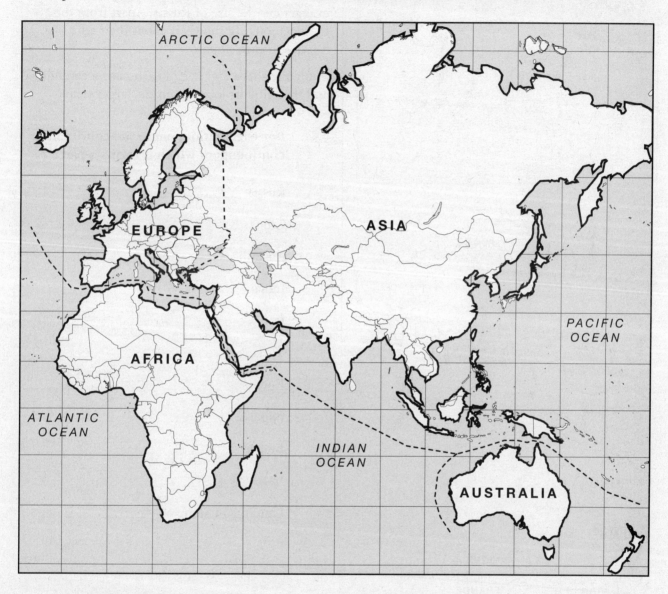

2 Which two continents are part of the same land mass?

A Africa and Asia

B Asia and Australia

C Europe and Africa

D Europe and Asia

3 Which continent does *not* border the Indian Ocean?

A Africa

B Asia

C Australia

D Europe

Here again is the map showing the continents of the Eastern Hemisphere.

Below it, you can see the outlines of eleven of the largest or politically most important nations shown on this map. The Mercator projection exaggerates the size of Russia. Apart from this, these nations are shown at about their true size, relative to each other.

Study the shape and size of each nation carefully, and then find its location on the larger map.

4 **For each nation, name the continent or continents of which it forms a part.**

Russia: _____

China: _____

Australia: _____

India: _____

Iran: _____

Turkey: _____

Egypt: _____

Nigeria: _____

France: _____

Iraq: _____

United Kingdom: _____

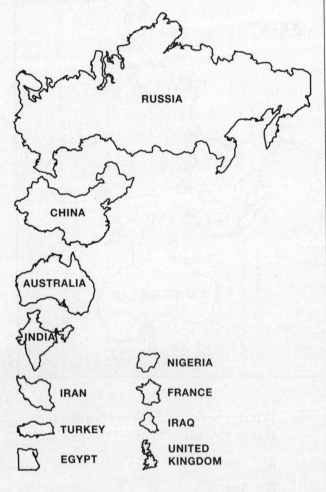

The Lands of the Western Hemisphere

This map shows the two continents of the Western Hemisphere. The dotted line separates the lands of North and South America.

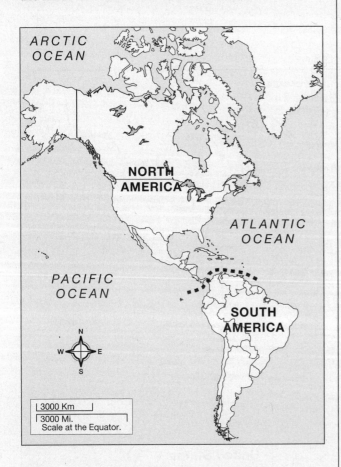

As in the map of the Eastern Hemisphere countries, the Mercator projection exaggerates the size of the land masses near the Poles, such as Canada and Greenland. Apart from this, the nations shown below are at about their true size, relative to each other. Study the shape and size of each nation and then find its location on the larger map.

5 Which ocean does *not* border any of the land masses in the Western Hemisphere?

A   Arctic Ocean

B   Atlantic Ocean

C   Indian Ocean

D   Pacific Ocean

6 For each nation, name the continent or continents of which it forms a part.

Canada: _____

Brazil: _____

Argentina: _____

Mexico: _____

Cuba: _____

THE UNITED STATES OF AMERICA

This political map shows the 50 states that make up the United States of America, along with the state capitals and other important cities. Note that Hawaii and Alaska are not to scale. Hawaii is smaller than it appears, and Alaska is much larger.

The map key explains the symbols used in the map.

Study the map carefully and answer the questions.

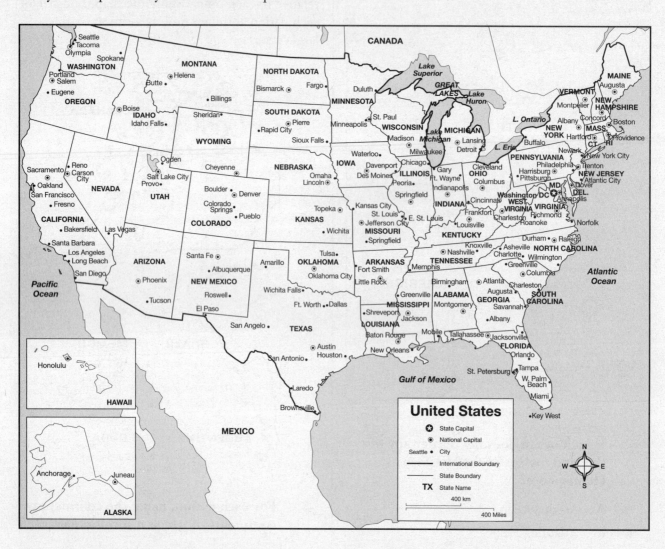

7 Which two states are closest to the national capital?

   A Delaware and West Virginia

   B Massachusetts and New York

   C New York and New Jersey

   D Virginia and Maryland (MD)

8 Which of the following cities is a state capital?

   A Chicago (Illinois)

   B Denver (Colorado)

   C New York City (New York)

   D Philadelphia (Pennsylvania)

9 Frankfort is the state capital of —

A Kentucky

B Minnesota

C Nevada

D New Jersey

10 Which of the following states lies on an international boundary?

A Iowa

B Louisiana

C New Mexico

D Tennessee

11 The Great Lakes —

A form a part of the boundary between the United States and Canada

B form a part of the boundary between the United States and Mexico

C form the Continental Divide between the western states and the eastern states

D lie at the most southerly point in the United States

12 Which is the northernmost city in the United States (excluding Alaska) shown on the map?

A Augusta

B Fargo

C Montpelier

D Seattle

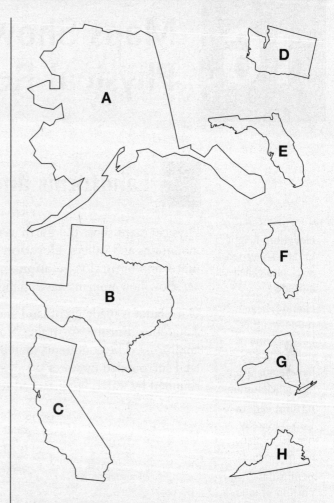

13 Study the outlines of eight of the largest or most populated states in the U.S. Identify each state on the lines below.

A: _____

B: _____

C: _____

D: _____

E: _____

F: _____

G: _____

H: _____

Maps Showing Physical Regions

Landforms and Water Forms

Physical maps show the Earth as nature made it. They include **landforms** like mountains and valleys, **elevation**—how far above or below sea level the land is, **climate**, and **natural vegetation**—what grows naturally in a region. Physical maps do *not* show how humans have changed the environment.

Our planet is made up of land and water. The seven continents: Asia, Africa, Antarctica, Europe, Australia, North America, and South America are Earth's main landforms. The continents include bodies of land and offshore islands. An island is land surrounded by water on all sides. A **peninsula** is a piece of land mostly surrounded by water, but attached to the mainland at one point.

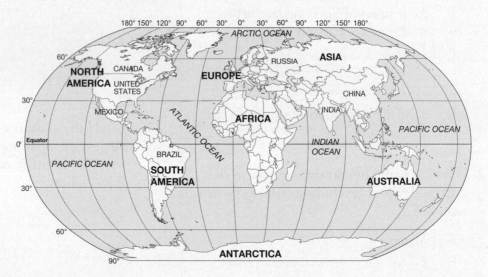

1 Which of the following is *not* a continent?

A   Africa

B   Antarctica

C   Arctica

D   Asia

Landforms cover only 30% of the earth's surface. The rest is water. The largest water forms are the oceans: the Atlantic, the Pacific, the Arctic, and the Indian Oceans. Seas, gulfs, and bays are also large bodies of water. Some seas and all gulfs and bays are parts of the oceans and lie near a coast. A **strait** is a narrow channel of water that lies between two larger bodies of water, usually oceans.

Other water bodies—a few seas and all rivers and lakes—are surrounded by land. Rivers usually rise in mountains and make their way to the open sea. The water in lakes and rivers is fresh, not salty.

The maps below show different land and water forms. Use them to answer the questions.

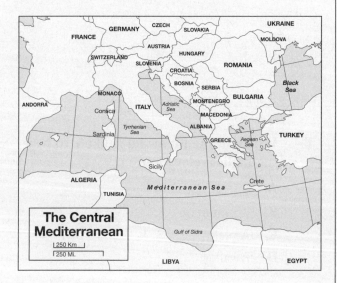

The Central Mediterranean

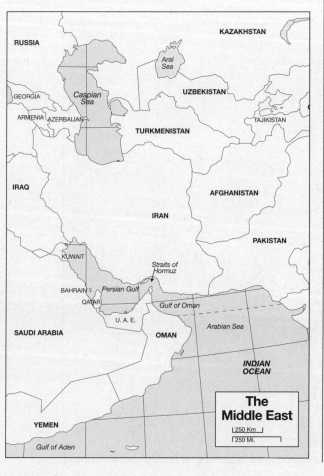

The Middle East

2 **Which of the following is a peninsula?**

A Albania

B Italy

C Sardinia

D Switzerland

3 **Which of the following is *not* an island?**

A Corsica

B Crete

C Romania

D Sicily

4 **Which two bodies of water are linked by the Straits of Hormuz?**

A Aegean Sea and Mediterranean Sea

B Indian Ocean and Gulf of Yemen

C Persian Gulf and Gulf of Oman

D Red Sea and Arabian Sea

5 **How does the Caspian Sea differ from the Mediterranean Sea?**

A It is surrounded by other bodies of water on all sides.

B It is surrounded by land on all sides.

C It links two bodies of water.

D It separates two peninsulas.

6 **What is the likely destination of an oil tanker that leaves the Indian Ocean and passes through the Gulf of Oman, the Straits of Hormuz, and up the Persian Gulf?**

A Afghanistan

B Iraq

C Oman

D Yemen

RELIEF MAPS

Relief maps show the surface of the Earth. Mostly this means high landforms like mountains, but it also includes valleys and plains. The name we give to a landform depends upon its shape and its elevation (height above sea level). The diagram below shows different-shaped landforms:

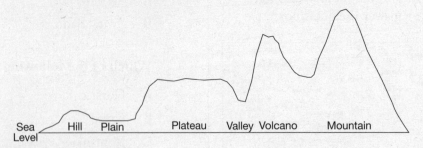

7 **What do plains and plateaus have in common?**

A   They are more or less flat.

B   They are hilly.

C   They are near sea level.

D   They rise to a peak.

8 **Which of the following is likely to have the highest elevation?**

A   A hill

B   A mountain

C   A plain

D   A valley

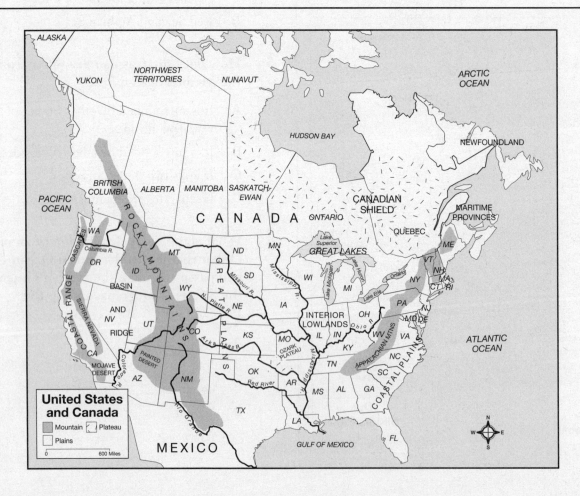

The map on the opposite page shows the land and water forms that make up the United States and Canada. Study the map and answer the questions.

9 **What kind of landform is the Canadian Shield?**

A Mountain

B Plain

C Plateau

D Valley

10 **What do you know about the region that lies in the west of North Dakota (ND), South Dakota (SD), Nebraska (NE), and Kansas (KS)?**

A It is fairly flat.

B It is below sea level.

C It is filled with high peaks.

D It lies between two mountain ranges.

11 **What is the name of the mountain range that runs from Canada down through the United States to the Mexican border?**

A Appalachians

B Cascades

C Coastal Range

D Rocky Mountains

12 **What do the Missouri River, the North Platte River, the Colorado River, and the Rio Grande have in common?**

A They flow into the Mississippi River.

B They flow west towards the Pacific Ocean.

C They form part of the boundary between the United States and Mexico.

D They have their source in the Rocky Mountains.

13 **Which of the following states does *not* border on the Great Lakes?**

A Iowa (IA)

B Michigan (MI)

C Minnesota (MN)

D Ohio (OH)

14 **Which two bodies of water shown on the map border on an ocean and lie in a coastal area?**

A Hudson Bay and the Gulf of Mexico

B Lake Erie and Lake Ontario

C Lake Superior and Lake Michigan

D The Columbia River and the Colorado River

15 **What does the map suggest about the east and west coasts of the United States?**

A Both coasts are fringed with high mountains.

B The east coast is hillier than the west coast.

C The region along the east coast is much closer to sea level than the region along the west coast.

D Unlike the west coast, the lands along the east coast lie below sea level.

16 **The Mississippi River forms a border between all of the following states *except* —**

A Arkansas (AR) and Mississippi (MS)

B Illinois (IL) and Missouri (MO)

C Iowa (IA) and Wisconsin (WI)

D Kentucky (KY) and Tennessee (TN)

ELEVATION

Unlike other relief maps, elevation maps do not distinguish among different kinds of landforms. They show only how far above or below sea level land lies. They show this by drawing rings around areas that lie within the same elevation range. The map key tells you what the shading patterns mean.

A question might ask:

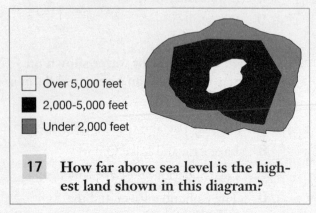

- [ ] Over 5,000 feet
- [■] 2,000-5,000 feet
- [■] Under 2,000 feet

17   How far above sea level is the highest land shown in this diagram?

The highest elevations in the diagram are shaded white. All the lands shaded white are more than 5,000 feet above sea level.

Now study this elevation map of the United States and answer the questions. You should also consult the relief map on page 150.

18   Which two states have the same elevation levels?

  A   Florida (FL) and Arizona (AZ)

  B   Minnesota (MN) and New Hampshire (NH)

  C   Ohio (OH) and Louisiana (LA)

  D   Oregon (OR) and Mississippi (MS)

19   How far above sea level are the eastern Coastal Plains?

  A   Under 700 feet

  B   Between 700 and 1,500 feet

  C   Between 1,501 and 7,000 feet

  D   Over 7,000 feet

20   Identify the lands between Montana (MT) and Texas (TX) that are over 7,000 feet high.

  A   Appalachians

  B   Great Plains

  C   Rocky Mountains

  D   Sierra Nevadas

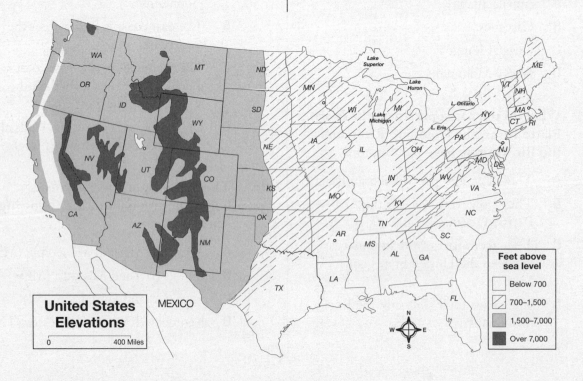

United States Elevations

0   400 Miles

MEXICO

Feet above sea level

- [ ] Below 700
- [▨] 700–1,500
- [▩] 1,500–7,000
- [■] Over 7,000

Natural Vegetation

The map below shows the world's natural vegetation regions. Remember that this shows what grows naturally in these regions. However, large areas of forest have been cut down and in many regions, cities and towns have been built on what used to be grassland. **Tundra** are the treeless plains found in very cold regions. The map includes some local names for different kinds of grassland.

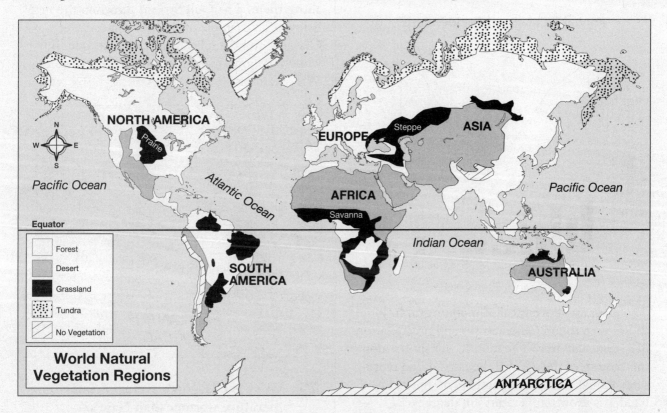

World Natural Vegetation Regions

Legend:
- Forest
- Desert
- Grassland
- Tundra
- No Vegetation

21 According to the map, Europe's natural vegetation is largely —

A desert

B forest

C grassland

D tundra

22 What kind of vegetation is to be found at the highest latitudes? (Remember that the highest latitudes are those furthest north and furthest south from the equator.)

A Desert

B Forest

C No vegetation

D Tundra

23 The northern half of which continent is largely desert?

A Africa

B Asia

C North America

D South America

GLOSSARY

tundra: vegetation region found in northern Russia and Arctic areas, consists of small plants

Climate

Climate refers to an area's average weather through the year; it also includes special events like hurricanes. The chief weather features are temperature and precipitation (rain or snow).

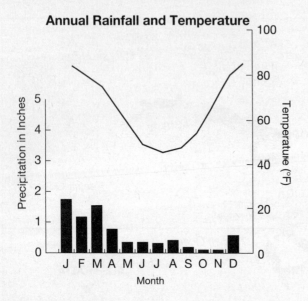

Annual Rainfall and Temperature

The diagram above is called a **climograph**. It shows year-round temperatures and precipitation in a particular area. The months are shown along the bottom of the graph. The curved line represents temperatures; the numbers on the right-hand axis show temperatures in degrees Fahrenheit. So, for the month of December, the average temperature is 85°F. The bars at the bottom of the graph show precipitation. The left-hand axis shows precipitation amounts in inches. The average rainfall in January totals a little under two inches.

24 What tells you that the climograph illustrates the climate in a region south of the equator? (Clue: winter comes to these regions during our summers.)

  A It is very wet in March.

  B January and December temperatures are about the same.

  C July and August are the coolest months.

  D October and November are quite dry.

Many factors contribute to climate. One of these is ocean currents. These are large movements of water pushed by the winds. When ocean currents move north from the tropics, they heat up the air above them. The Gulf Stream shown in the map below is an example of this. As you can see, Glasgow and Nain lie at the same latitude. But while Glasgow's average winter temperature is 39°F, Nain's is -7°F.

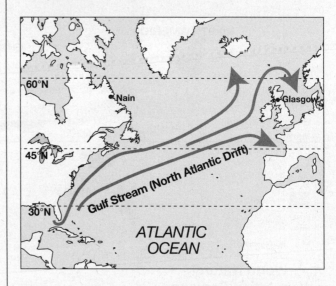

25 **Why is Glasgow's average winter temperature warmer than Nain's?**

  A Glasgow is closer to the equator.

  B Glasgow lies south of the equator, so its winter is our summer.

  C The Gulf Stream has warmed the Atlantic waters that flow near Glasgow, and this has warmed the air above, too.

  D Glasgow lies on the eastern side of an ocean and temperatures are always warmer in the east than in the west.

GLOSSARY

climograph: graph used to show year-round temperatures and precipitation at a single location, usually a city

Three more factors that affect climate are latitude, **altitude**, and landform barriers. You have seen how latitude affects climate: areas close to the equator are the hottest and those close to the poles are coldest. The further above sea level you go, the colder it gets. Mount Kenya in Africa lies on the equator, so you would expect it to be very hot. But its peak is 17,058 feet above sea level, and it is covered with ice. Landforms such as high mountain ranges act as barriers—they block the movement of air. Mountains may block moisture-bearing western winds from traveling eastward.

The climate map of Asia shows these factors at work. It shows how the climate grows colder as you move north from the equator. It also shows that mountain regions are cooler than flatter areas. The Himalayan Mountains prevent the cold winter air of Central Asia from reaching India, giving the Indian subcontinent a year-round tropical climate.

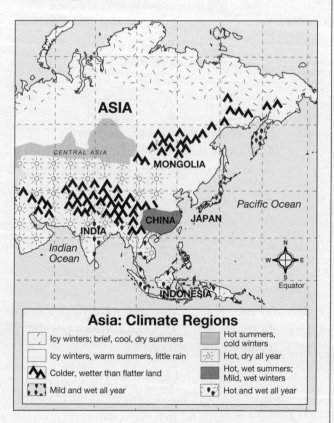

Asia: Climate Regions

- Icy winters; brief, cool, dry summers
- Icy winters, warm summers, little rain
- Colder, wetter than flatter land
- Mild and wet all year
- Hot summers, cold winters
- Hot, dry all year
- Hot, wet summers; Mild, wet winters
- Hot and wet all year

26 What factor **best** explains Indonesia's climate?

A   Altitude

B   Landform barriers

C   Latitude

D   Ocean currents

27 Why is the winter climate in northern India warmer than the climate in those parts of China that lie at the same latitudes?

A   Because India lies further south

B   Because the Indian Ocean currents warm the mainland

C   Because mountains prevent cool air from reaching northern India

D   Because India lies at a lower altitude

28 Tibet is a mountainous region that lies between India and China. What kind of climate does it have?

A   Hot, wet summers and mild, wet winters

B   Icy winters and brief dry, cool summers

C   Icy winters and warm dry summers

D   Its climate is cooler and wetter than the flatter land nearby.

GLOSSARY

altitude: elevation, height of land above sea level

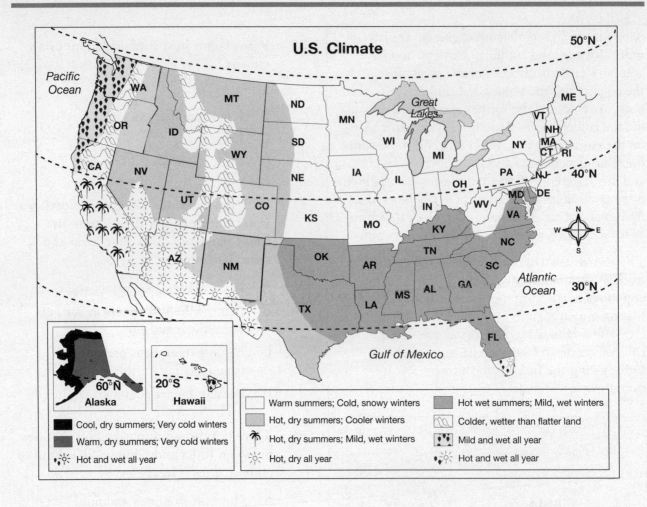

U.S. Climate

Legend:
- Cool, dry summers; Very cold winters
- Warm, dry summers; Very cold winters
- Hot and wet all year
- Warm summers; Cold, snowy winters
- Hot, dry summers; Cooler winters
- Hot, dry summers; Mild, wet winters
- Hot, dry all year
- Hot wet summers; Mild, wet winters
- Colder, wetter than flatter land
- Mild and wet all year
- Hot and wet all year

This map shows how different factors influence the U.S. climate. Use it to answer the following questions.

29 The different climates of Alaska and Hawaii can largely be explained by —

A altitude

B latitude

C landforms

D ocean currents

30 Which state has the coldest winters?

A Delaware (DE)

B Kansas (KS)

C Kentucky (KY)

D North Carolina (NC)

31 The coastal regions of Southern California lie at about the same latitude as Arizona. How does the climate differ?

A Arizona is much cooler.

B Arizona is much drier.

C Arizona is much wetter.

D Arizona is both cooler and wetter.

32 What explains the climate difference between Southern California's coastal regions and Arizona?

A Arizona lies further north.

B Arizona's mountains make its climate colder and wetter.

C High mountains ranges prevent moisture moving east from California.

D Ocean currents make California cooler.

Landform, Vegetation, and Climate

Landforms, natural vegetation, and climate impact one another. Compare these two maps of South America. As you can see, most of the north/northeastern part of the continent has a tropical climate—it is hot and wet all year. Most of the vegetation in this area is tropical forest. Hot damp weather is ideal for rainforest trees—the climate is largely responsible for what grows in this region.

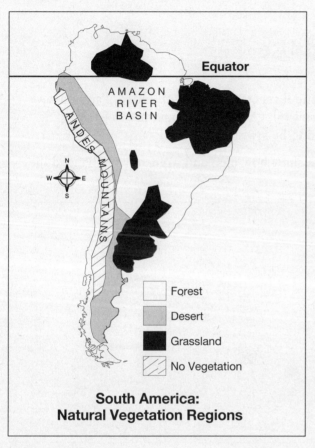

South America: Natural Vegetation Regions

Legend:
- Forest
- Desert
- Grassland
- No Vegetation

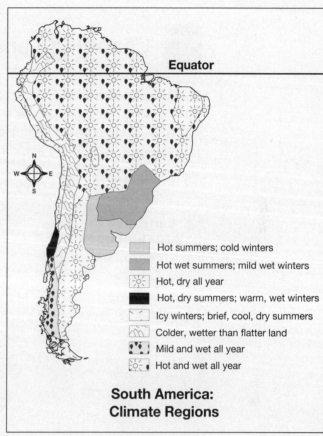

South America: Climate Regions

Legend:
- Hot summers; cold winters
- Hot wet summers; mild wet winters
- Hot, dry all year
- Hot, dry summers; warm, wet winters
- Icy winters; brief, cool, dry summers
- Colder, wetter than flatter land
- Mild and wet all year
- Hot and wet all year

33 Can you find another area in South America where the boundaries of a natural vegetation region are similar to those of a climate region? Explain how landform and climate might affect vegetation in this region.

_____

_____

_____

_____

_____

_____

Maps and Graphs Showing Human Activity and Geography

Changing Land Use

In many parts of the world, the natural vegetation has disappeared. Farmers have cleared forests to make way for farmland. Citizens have built housing, shopping centers, and factories on what used to be grassland.

Land use maps, like the one below, show how men and women have changed the Earth's surface.

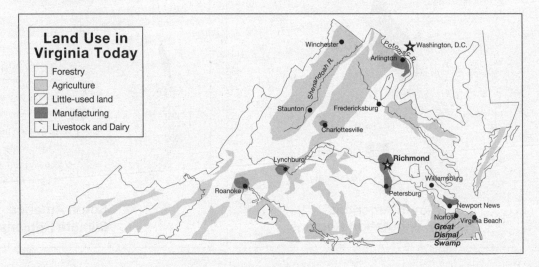

Land Use in Virginia Today
- ☐ Forestry
- ☐ Agriculture
- ☐ Little-used land
- ■ Manufacturing
- ☐ Livestock and Dairy

Winchester • Washington, D.C. ☆
Arlington
Staunton • Fredericksburg •
Charlottesville •
Lynchburg • Richmond ☆
Roanoke • Williamsburg
Petersburg • Newport News
Norfolk • Virginia Beach
Great Dismal Swamp
Shenandoah R.
Potomac R.

---

1 The land around the Shenandoah River is mainly used for —

A agriculture

B dairy farming

C manufacturing

D recreation and tourism

2 What kind of land use is <u>most</u> similar to natural vegetation? Put another way, which of the following is used by humans and also occurs naturally?

A Agriculture

B Dairy farming

C Forestry

D Manufacturing

Agriculture, Industry, and Mining

You will come across different types of product maps in your texts and on social studies tests. Some will be general land-use maps like the one opposite and show the different kinds of economic activity in a region. Others will concentrate on certain kinds of activity, such as agriculture or industry.

The map below shows farming and forestry in the Midwest. It shows the kinds of crops that are grown and the animals that are raised in different sections of the Midwest.

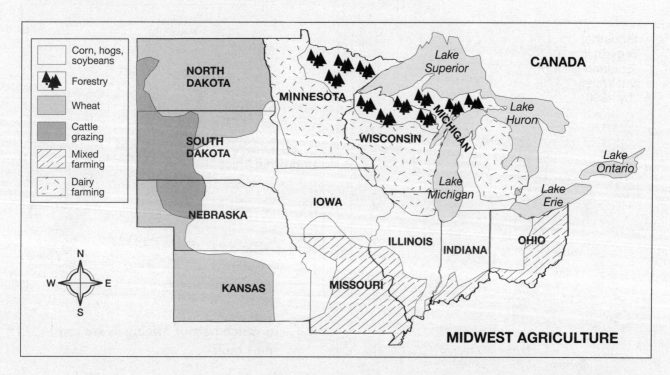

MIDWEST AGRICULTURE

3 Forestry is a major activity in all of the following states *except* —

A   Illinois

B   Michigan

C   Minnesota

D   Wisconsin

4 In which section of the Midwest is cattle grazing <u>most</u> widespread?

A   The northeast

B   The northwest

C   The southeast

D   The southwest

5 Which of the following is a major milk-, butter-, and cheese-producing state?

A   Iowa

B   Kansas

C   Ohio

D   Wisconsin

6 What crop is grown in a wide stretch of land running east-west through the center of the region?

A   Corn

B   Cotton

C   Rice

D   Wheat

The first major change in land use came about with the spread of farming. Before this, much of the world was covered with forests. The second big change was the result of industrialization. The early nineteenth century saw the building of mills and factories in England. Industry swiftly spread to parts of the European continent and to the United States.

The earliest U.S. factories were New England's cotton mills. The years after the Civil War saw the growth of coal mining and steel manufacturing. In the twentieth century, plants opened up across the Northeast and Midwest to manufacture food products, electrical appliances, automobiles, and other industrial goods.

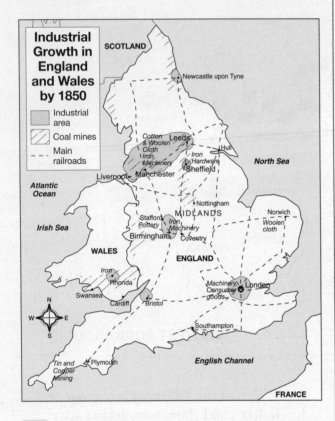

7 **The map shows areas of coal-mining and newly built factories. In what other way does it show how the English landscape changed during the nineteenth century?**

A Lakes were turned into reservoirs.

B Large forests were cleared.

C Much of the land became unusable as a result of heavy wartime bombing.

D Railroad tracks began to criss-cross the country.

8 **In which part of Michigan are most ships built?**

A Along the shore of Lake Michigan

B Along the southern border

C In the Southeast along the shore of Lake Huron

D The Upper Peninsula

9 **Based on the map, what industry would you suppose was the key to Michigan's industrial growth?**

A Automobile manufacture

B Machinery

C Military supplies

D Textiles

RESOURCE MAPS

Fertile soil, large trees, and clean water are all valuable resources. But the kind of resources you will often find on a map are those that lie under-ground, especially minerals and fuels.

Minerals include precious metals like gold and silver, metals with industrial uses like copper and tin, and salts and other minerals that are used in foods and medicines. Fuels include oil, coal, and natural gas, and also fast-moving streams whose energy is converted into hydroelectric power. Oil products are used not only to power automobiles, they are also used to produce fertilizers and other goods.

10 **What resource is found in Michigan's Upper Peninsula?**

A   Iron ore

B   Natural gas

C   Oil

D   Salt

11 **Look at the industry map of Michigan on the opposite page. Choose two industries. Identify any of the resources shown below or in the Midwest map on page 159 that are used in those industries.**

_____

_____

_____

_____

_____

_____

_____

_____

_____

Michigan Resources and Land Use

- Iron and copper
- Forests
- Salt
- Corn, soybeans, wheat, sugar beets, and hogs
- Fruit & vegetable farming
- Dairy farming
- Oil and natural gas wells

Lake Michigan

Lake Huron

Population Statistics

Population maps use different shading to show **population density**—how many people live in a particular region. These maps show the population of cities, states, regions, countries, hemispheres, and the whole world. Many population maps, including the one below, tell you how many people live in a square mile or a square kilometer.

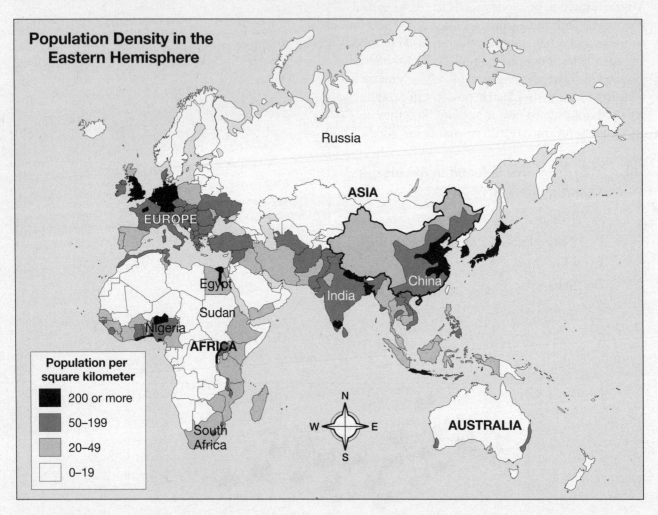

Population Density in the Eastern Hemisphere

Russia

ASIA

EUROPE

Egypt

Sudan

Nigeria

India

China

AFRICA

Population per square kilometer

200 or more

50–199

20–49

0–19

South Africa

N W E S

AUSTRALIA

12 Which of the following areas has over 200 inhabitants per square kilometer?

A East Africa

B Northeastern China

C Southern Europe

D Western Australia

GLOSSARY

population density: the number of people who live in a given area

13 Of the four African nations identified on the map, which one has fewer than 20 people per square kilometer?

A Egypt

B Nigeria

C South Africa

D Sudan

MEASURING POPULATION SUBGROUPS

Population maps count not only how many people, but also what kind of people. For a given area, historians may measure the population according to race, religion, ethnic group, or income. The map below examines the populations of Pennsylvania, New York, Delaware, and New Jersey in colonial times.

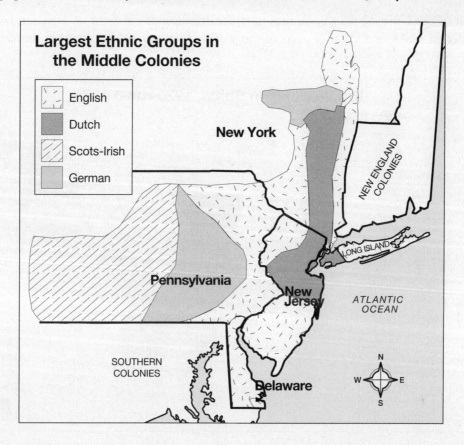

14 The map above distinguishes the inhabitants of the Middle Colonies on the basis of —

A the color of their skin

B the countries they or their ancestors came from

C the jobs they held

D the religious groups they belonged to

15 The people of western Pennsylvania were largely—

A Dutch

B English

C German

D Scots-Irish

16 In which colony were most of the inhabitants from one ethnic group?

A Delaware

B New Jersey

C New York

D Pennsylvania

POPULATION CHANGE

Populations change. Disease, war, and human migration and immigration can raise or reduce the number of people living in a given area. With the coming of industrialization, millions of people left the farms and moved to cities to find factory jobs.

The population of the United States continues to shift. Immigrants continue to arrive in large numbers from Latin America and Asia and other parts of the world. The map below shows how state populations changed between 1970 and 1990.

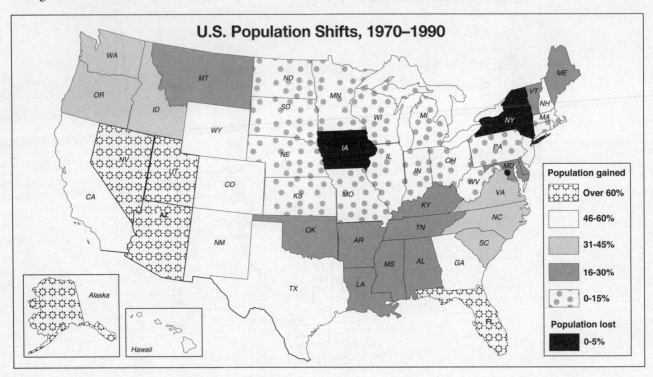

U.S. Population Shifts, 1970–1990

17 In which of the following states did the population increase by the largest percentage between 1970 and 1990?

A Alaska

B Kansas (KS)

C New Mexico (NM)

D Oregon (OR)

18 Declining industry in the Northeast helps to explain the population decline in —

A Iowa (IA)

B New Hampshire (NH)

C New York (NY)

D Virginia (VA)

19 How might climate help to explain the population gains in states like Florida (FL) and Arizona (AZ)? (You may want to consult the climate map on page 156)

_____

_____

_____

_____

_____

_____

_____

GRAPHS OF POPULATION STATISTICS

Geographers and historians use graphs as well as maps to show population statistics.

The bar chart below shows how the world's largest metropolitan areas (cities and their suburbs) grew over a thirty-year period ending in 2000. Given the rapid population growth in the developing world, it is not surprising to find most of the largest population increases in the Third World. Notice in particular that New York, the only older industrial area shown, is also the only one that lost population in this period.

20 Which metropolitan area had the largest population increase between 1971 and 2000?

A   Bombay

B   Mexico City

C   Teheran

D   Tokyo

The line graph below shows how the world's population grew between 1750 and 2000, and how it is projected to grow over the next fifty years.

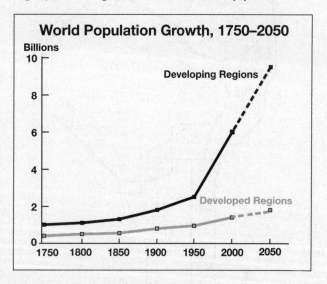

21 In which 50-year period did the population in developing regions almost triple?

A   1750-1800

B   1850-1900

C   1900-1950

D   1950-2000

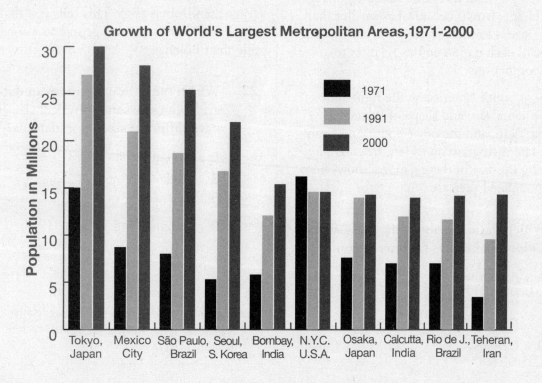

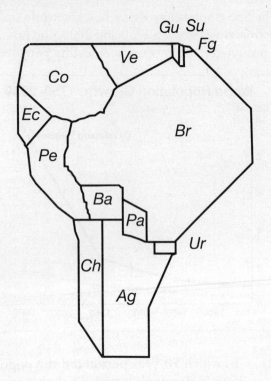

The graph above is called a **cartogram**. Cartograms alter the size of an area. They do this in order to show something else about the area. This could be the number of people who live there. Densely populated nations would be shown as larger than their true size. Regions with few inhabitants would be shown as smaller than their true size. However, cartograms try to keep the shape of each nation and its relation to neighboring nations.

The map of South America on the right above shows the actual size and shape of Brazil, Argentina, Peru, and the other South American nations. The cartogram on its left, by enlarging or reducing the size of these nations, shows how densely populated they are.

22 **Which nation is about the same size as Colombia but has far fewer people?**

A Argentina

B Bolivia

C Paraguay

D Uruguay

The answer is Bolivia. If you compare Columbia and Bolivia on the right-hand map, you can see that they are roughly the same size. But the map on the left shows Colombia (Co) as much larger than Bolivia (Ba). This tells you that Colombia has many more people to a square mile than Bolivia.

23 **Which other South American nations are about the same physical size but have different sized populations?**

A Argentina and Brazil

B Chile and French Guyana

C Ecuador and Suriname

D Uruguay and Venezuela

GLOSSARY

cartogram: a type of map that shows relative scale of something other than physical size—such as population density.

So far we have discussed population mainly in terms of size. There are two other important ways to look at a population—by gender and by age.

Suppose an economist wants to calculate how much money the Social Security system will need to spend on pensions over the next 20 years. He or she will need to know how many retired people there will be during that period. Or suppose a local government wants to see if they will have enough schools and classrooms over the next five years. Officials will need to know how many children will reach school age, as well as how many students are already attending school.

Population pyramids show the age and gender of a population. That is, they show what proportion of the population is male or female, and young, middle-aged, or elderly.

The population of Mexico is shown in the graph on the right. At the bottom of the graph you can see population percentages. The lightly shaded blocks on the left represent the male population, and the darker blocks on the right represent females. The graph shows that at all ages, half the Mexican population is male and half is female. At the left of the graph you can see age ranges. They tell you what percentage are males and females between the ages of zero and four, five and nine, and so on. You can see that 16 percent (eight percent male and eight percent female) of the Mexican population is less than five years old. On the other hand, less than one percent is aged 80 or more.

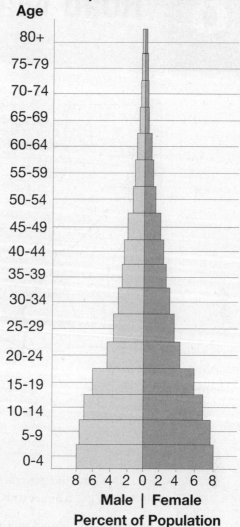

Age Structure of the Population of Mexico

Male | Female
Percent of Population

24 **About what percentage of the Mexican population are males aged between 25 and 29?**

A   About one percent

B   About two percent

C   About three percent

D   About four percent

To find the correct answer you need to find the age range 25-29 at the left and then look to the right at the lighter blocks that represent young men. The numbers at the bottom tell you that four percent of male Mexicans are in this category.

25 **About four percent of Mexicans are aged between —**

A   five and nine

B   25 and 29

C   45 and 49

D   75 and 79

GLOSSARY

population pyramid: graph used to show structure of a population according to age and gender

18 Road Maps

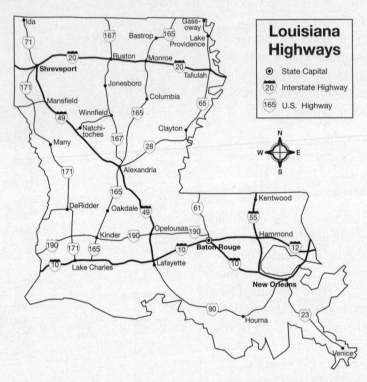

Most maps provide general information. Road maps have a particular goal—to tell you how to get from A to B.

The map above shows you the major highways of the state of Louisiana. The most important roads are the interstate highways that criss-cross the United States. East-west interstates have even numbers and north-south interstates have odd numbers. The map also shows U.S. highways. A more detailed road map would also show state highways and county and town roads.

1 **Which cities are linked by Interstate 20?**

A Baton Rouge and Lafayette   C Opelousas and Alexandria

B Kentwood and Hammond   D Shreveport and Tallulah

2 **Which are the <u>most</u> direct routes between the city of Venice in south-eastern Louisiana and the state capital?**

A Highway 23 and Interstate 10   C Highway 23 and Highway 90

B Highway 23 and Interstate 12   D Interstate 12 and Interstate 10

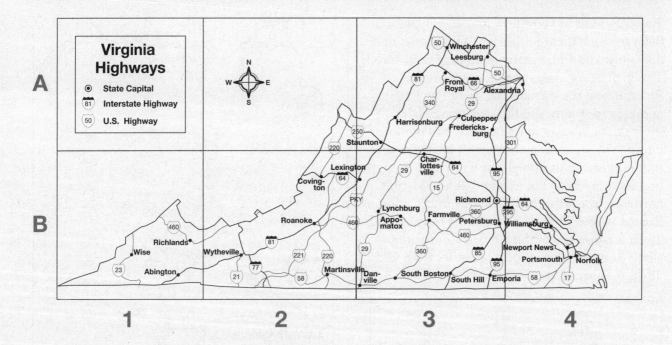

Many road maps include grid systems. Like the lines of latitude and longitude, grids can help you locate places on a map. Grids divide a map into boxes. In this map of Virginia, each box is identified by a letter and a number. Suppose you needed to travel from Richmond, Virginia to the town of Wise. If you don't know the location of Wise, you could look up a map index.

W	
Williamsburg	B4
Winchester	A3
Wise	B1
Wytheville	B2

Now that you know that Wise is in the square B1, it is easy to find it on the map. Use the map index below to help you find South Hill on the map.

R	
Richlands	B1
Richmond	B3
Roanoke	B2
S	
South Boston	B3
South Hill	B3
Staunton	A3

3 Which square contains Charlottesville, Danville, and Emporia?

A   A3

B   B2

C   B3

D   B4

4 Which interstate highways link Norfolk in southeastern Virginia and Winchester in the northern part of the state?

A   I-64 and I-81

B   I-95, I-295, and I-64

C   I-95 and I-77,

D   I-95, I-66, and I-85

5 Which city does *not* lie along Route 58?

A   Danville

B   Emporia

C   Martinsville

D   Wytheville

Travelers want to know how long it will take them to reach their destination. This means that they must know how many miles they must travel. The map below shows the made-up town of Riverton and the surrounding area. The larger numbers are routes and the smaller numbers show the number of miles between two points of interest. (A point of interest might be where two routes intersect, or it might be a town, or it might be a highway exit.) For example, Route 52 runs northeast from Riverton. From the intersection of Routes 52 and 75 in Riverton to the town of Old Town is a distance of three miles. Continuing along Route 52, it is three more miles from Old Town to Tower Lake.

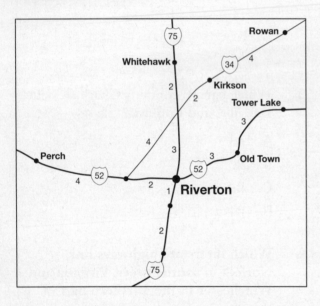

6 If you entered Route 75 where it intersects Route 52, how many miles north would you drive to reach Whitehawk?

A Two miles

B Five miles

C Six miles

D Nine miles

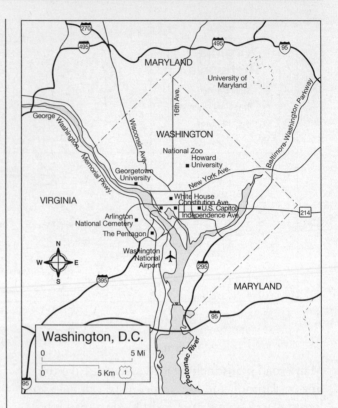

City maps are usually much more than just street maps. Like this map of Washington, D.C., they also show historical sites, public buildings, and airports.

7 The Potomac River forms the western and southwestern border of Washington, D.C. Which of the following lies in the city?

A Arlington National Cemetery

B Georgetown University

C The Pentagon

D Washington National Airport

8 In what direction from Washington would you expect Baltimore to lie? (Clue: which way does the Baltimore-Washington Parkway go?)

A East

B Northeast

C Southwest

D West

Unit Review

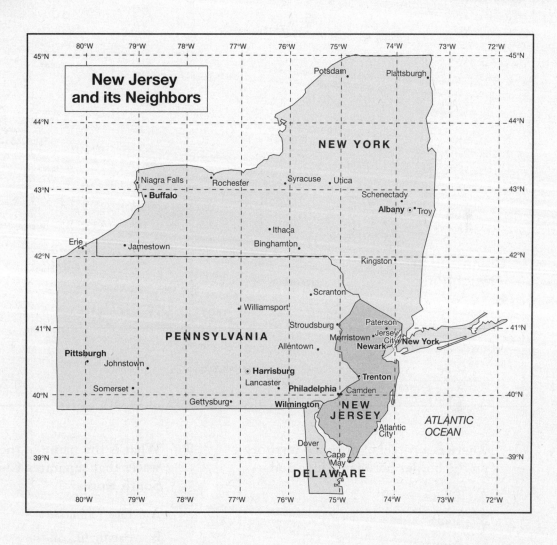

New Jersey and its Neighbors

(Map showing New York, Pennsylvania, New Jersey, and Delaware with cities including Potsdam, Plattsburgh, Niagra Falls, Rochester, Syracuse, Utica, Buffalo, Schenectady, Albany, Troy, Ithaca, Binghamton, Erie, Jamestown, Kingston, Scranton, Williamsport, Stroudsburg, Paterson, Jersey City, Morristown, New York, Newark, Allentown, Pittsburgh, Johnstown, Harrisburg, Lancaster, Trenton, Somerset, Gettysburg, Philadelphia, Camden, Wilmington, Atlantic City, Dover, Cape May, and the Atlantic Ocean)

---

1 Which city is closest to the intersection of 75°W and 39°N?

A Cape May

B Dover

C Philadelphia

D Wilmington

2 Which two states shown on the map share a border with the other three states?

F Delaware and Pennsylvania

G New Jersey and New York

H New York and Delaware

J Pennsylvania and New Jersey

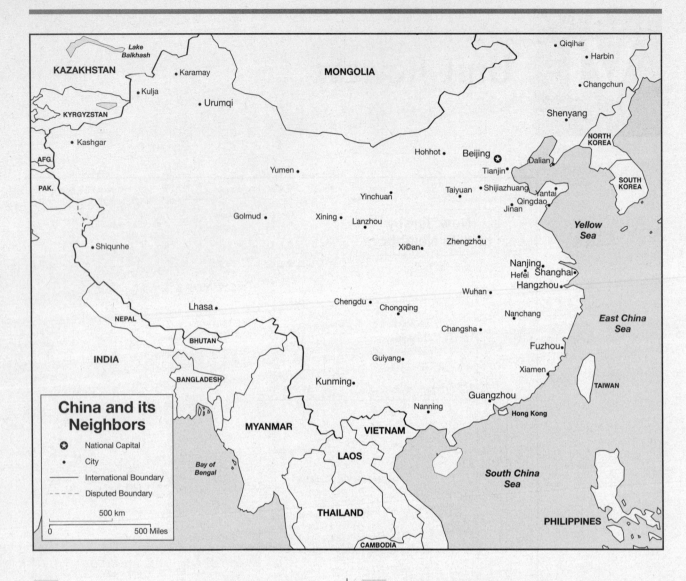

China and its Neighbors

National Capital

City

International Boundary

Disputed Boundary

500 km

0   500 Miles

3 There is a parcel of disputed territory on the border between China and —

A   Bhutan

B   India

C   Mongolia

D   Myanmar

4 What is the capital of China?

F   Beijing

G   Hong Kong

H   Nanjing

J   Shanghai

5 What is the name of the body of water that separates China from South Korea?

A   East China Sea

B   Pacific Ocean

C   South China Sea

D   Yellow Sea

6 Which of the following nations does *not* lie along China's southern border?

F   Laos

G   Myanmar

H   Thailand

J   Vietnam

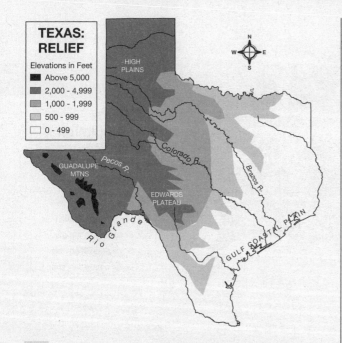

TEXAS: RELIEF

Elevations in Feet
Above 5,000
2,000 - 4,999
1,000 - 1,999
500 - 999
0 - 499

HIGH PLAINS

GUADALUPE MTNS

Pecos R.

Colorado R.

EDWARDS PLATEAU

Brazos R.

Rio Grande

GULF COASTAL PLAIN

7   **Where is the highest land in Texas?**

A   Along the Edwards Plateau

B   In the Guadalupe Mountains

C   In the Texas High Plains

D   On the Gulf Coast

8   **How many feet above sea level is the Gulf Coastal Plain?**

F   Under 500 feet

G   Between 500 and 1,000 feet

H   Between 1,000 and 2,000 feet

J   Over five thousand feet

9   **Write the name of these four countries on the line to the right of each one.**

_____

_____

_____

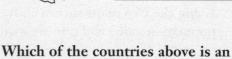

_____

10   **Which of the countries above is an island?**

_____

11   **The Atlantic Ocean lies off the eastern coast of which of the countries shown above?**

_____

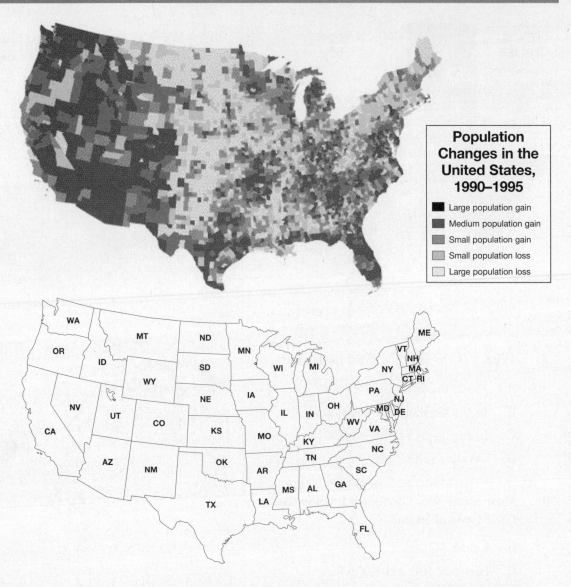

Population Changes in the United States, 1990–1995

- ■ Large population gain
- ■ Medium population gain
- ■ Small population gain
- □ Small population loss
- □ Large population loss

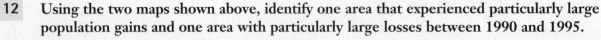

12 Using the two maps shown above, identify one area that experienced particularly large population gains and one area with particularly large losses between 1990 and 1995.

_____

_____

_____

13 Give one reason to account for these population losses and one to account for population gains.

_____

_____

_____

VII Practice Test

Museum of the City of New York

Immigrants cross the Atlantic on S.S. Pennland

1 In about which year would you guess the photograph above was taken?

A 1700

B 1800

C 1900

D 2000

2 Where do you think these immigrants were coming from?

F Canada

G Central and South America

H East Asia

J Southern and Eastern Europe

3 What conclusion about these immigrants can you draw from the photo and why?

_____

_____

_____

_____

_____

_____

_____

175

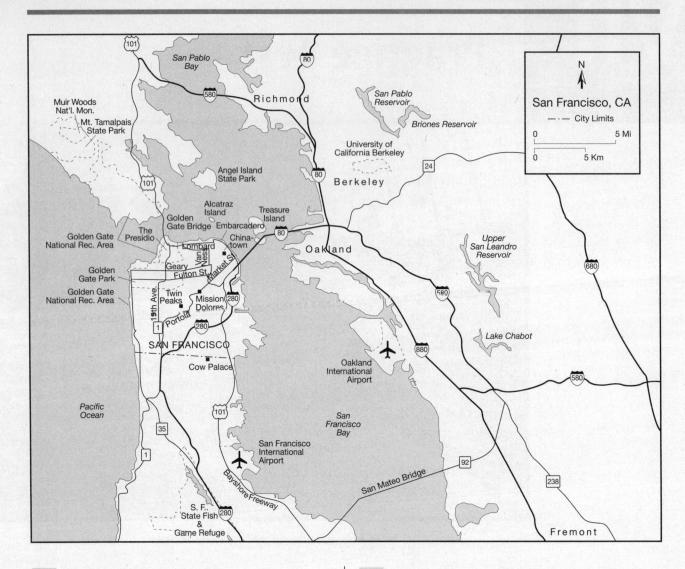

4 The map suggests that San Francisco—

F can be reached only by ferry

G is land-locked

H lies at the tip of a peninsula

J lies on an island

5 Three highways cross San Francisco Bay and San Pablo Bay. Which of the following is *not* one of them?

A I-80

B I-280

C I-580

D Route 92

6 Which of the following lies outside San Francisco's city limits?

F Chinatown

G Golden Gate Park

H Mission Dolores

J The University of California at Berkeley

7 How many miles by road is San Francisco from the Oakland International Airport?

A About eight miles

B About 18 miles

C About 28 miles

D About 38 miles

> It was agreed that Henry Wakelee shall watch over the youths or any disorderly carriages in the time of public worship on the Lord's day or other time and see that they behave themselves comely and note any disorderly persons by such raps or blows as he in his discretion shall see meet.
>
> *Town records of Stratford, Connecticut*

8 **What tells you that both the documents on this page are primary sources?**

F Both are written documents, as opposed to speeches or drawings.

G Both involve careful planning rather than knee-jerk reactions.

H Both refer to events in the distant past.

J Both were created by individuals who took part in or witnessed events.

9 **What do both documents have in common?**

A They show a government making a decision for the community.

B They show how important religion was in colonial New England.

C They show that small-town neighbors ignored each other's problems.

D They show the role that accidents can play in human life.

10 **What does the word *comely* mean as it is used in the passage above?**

F Charmingly

G Noisily

H Pretty

J Properly

> About noon the chimney of Mr. Sharp's house in Boston took fire, the splinters being not clayed at the top, and taking the thatch burnt it down, and the wind being N.W., drove the fire to Mr. Colburn's house and burnt that down also, yet they saved most of their goods...
>
> For the prevention whereof in our new town, intended this summer to be builded, we have ordered that no man there shall build his chimney with wood, nor cover his house with thatch, which was readily assented unto, for that divers other houses have been burned since our arrival.
>
> *Governor John Winthrop of Massachusetts, writing in his journal in 1630*

11 **What was Governor Winthrop's main concern?**

A That citizens needed to build a new and better town

B That citizens protect their homes

C That so many houses were burning down

D That the climate was making it difficult for the people of Boston to survive

12 **How did Governor Winthrop hope to avoid similar problems in the future?**

F By abandoning the city of Boston and building a new town

G By banning the use of certain building materials

H By requiring that all new building take place in the winter when there was less risk of fire

J By requiring that houses be built further apart from each other

Components of Exported Goods and Services
(2000 Annual Data)

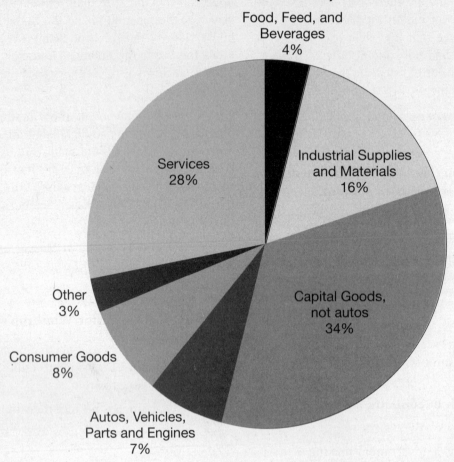

Food, Feed, and Beverages 4%

Industrial Supplies and Materials 16%

Services 28%

Capital Goods, not autos 34%

Other 3%

Consumer Goods 8%

Autos, Vehicles, Parts and Engines 7%

---

13 Based upon the pie chart above, which statement is likely to be correct?

A The majority of U.S. exports consist of military equipment.

B The United States imports more goods than it exports.

C The United States is the world's largest exporter of foodstuffs and machinery.

D The United States produces a food surplus.

14 Apart from capital goods, the largest category of U.S. exports is —

F auto-related items

G consumer goods

H services

J supplies and materials

Population Density of New Jersey Counties in 1990

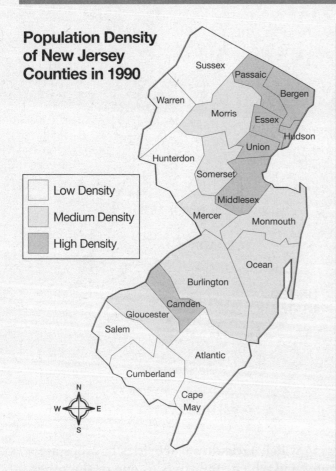

Legend:
- Low Density
- Medium Density
- High Density

Age Structure of the Population of Germany in 1985

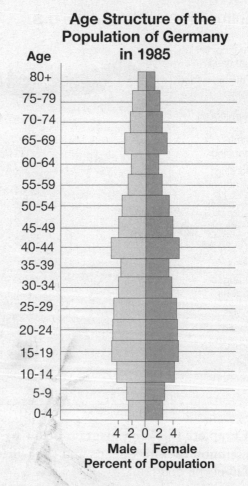

Male | Female
Percent of Population

---

15 Counties near large cities have larger populations than those in more rural areas. Which New Jersey counties lie closest to New York City?

A Atlantic, Cumberland, and Cape May

B Bergen, Hudson, and Union

C Burlington, Camden, and Gloucester

D Ocean, Middlesex, and Monmouth

16 What would you guess is the main economic activity in Hunterdon County?

F Farming

G Manufacturing

H Mining

J Service industry

17 What percentage of Germans were aged over 70 in 1985?

A About two percent

B About six percent

C About 12 percent

D About 22 percent

18 Germany lost a large percentage of its male population during World War II (1939-1945). How does the graph show this?

F The birth rate declined between 1940 and 1950.

G The birth rate rose after 1980.

H There are fewer men than women aged over 65 (those of fighting age in 1945).

J There was a baby boom around 1960.

Agriculture in Canada and the U.S.

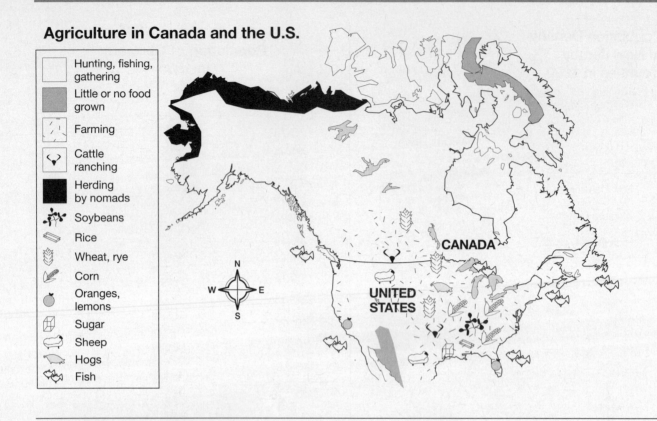

Legend:
- Hunting, fishing, gathering
- Little or no food grown
- Farming
- Cattle ranching
- Herding by nomads
- Soybeans
- Rice
- Wheat, rye
- Corn
- Oranges, lemons
- Sugar
- Sheep
- Hogs
- Fish

19 Complete the Venn diagram below by showing which agricultural activities or crops are common to both Canada and the United States and which apply only to one or the other. Label the diagram.

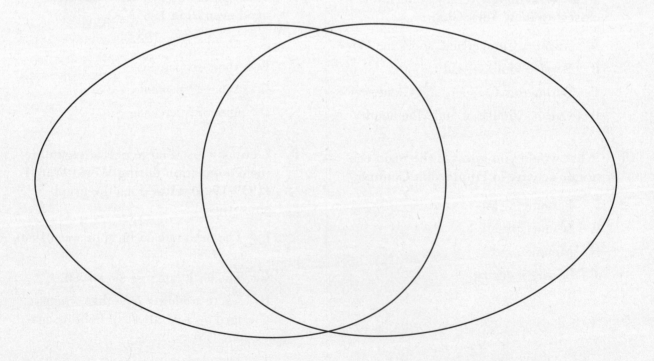

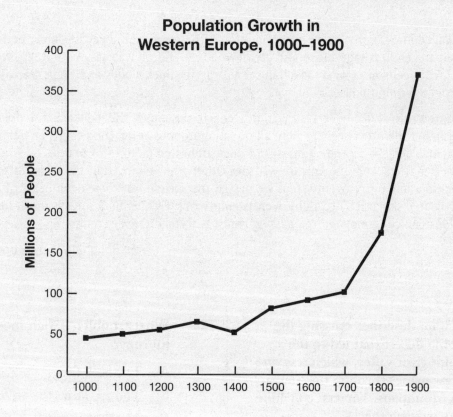

Population Growth in Western Europe, 1000–1900

Millions of People

20 About how many people lived in Western Europe in 1900?

F 375,000

G Three and a half million

H 375,000,000

J 375 billion

21 You have read about the impact of the Black Death and the Industrial Revolution on population levels. At which two dates can you see this? That is, in which year can you detect a population decline caused by the former, and in which year can you detect the start of the population increase caused by the latter?

A 1200 and 1600

B 1300 and 1700

C 1400 and 1800

D 1500 and 1900

{We} were walled in by barren, snow-clad mountains, There was not a tree in sight. There was no vegetation but the endless sage-brush and greasewood. All nature was gray with it. We were ploughing through great deeps of powdery alkali dust that rose in thick clouds and floated across the plain, like smoke from a burning house.

...We were coated with it like millers; so were the coach, the mules, the mailbags, the driver—we and the sage-brush and the other scenery were all one monotonous color. Long trains of freight wagons in the distances enveloped in ascending masses of dust suggested pictures of prairies on fire. These teams and their masters were the only life we saw. Otherwise we moved in the midst of solitude, silence, and desolation. Every twenty steps we passed the skeleton of some dead beast of burthen, with its dust-coated skin stretched tight over its empty ribs. Frequently a solemn raven sat upon the skull or the hips and contemplated the passing coach with meditative serenity.

From Roughing It *by Mark Twain, 1872*

22 Mark Twain describes crossing the Forty-Mile desert that led to the Humboldt river valley, which was one of the few passes through the Sierra Nevada Mountains. You can conclude from the passage that —

F most travelers preferred to use SUVs rather than mule trains

G the mountains created an impassable obstacle for travelers

H this was a fertile farming area

J this was the route was taken by most wagon trains

23 What troubled Twain <u>most</u> about this journey?

A The bush fires

B The dry heat

C The dust

D The emptiness of the landscape

From The Wasp, *published in San Francisco in 1888*

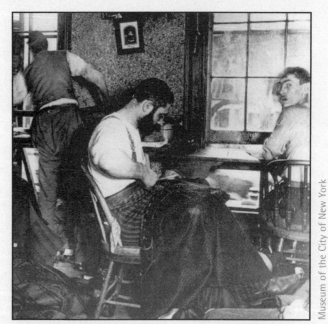

Sweatshop on Hester Street, New York City

24 **What is happening in the cartoon shown above?**

F Two figures are playing outside a high stone arch.

G Uncle Sam has stolen a letter from the dragon.

H Uncle Sam is kicking a dragon into the water.

J Uncle Sam is trying to save the life of a dragon which is falling into the water.

25 **The dragon in the drawing symbolizes the Chinese. What is the message of this cartoon?**

A Americans living on the West Coast did not welcome Chinese immigrants.

B Americans were concerned about the fact that most Chinese immigrants did not speak English.

C San Francisco's white and Asian populations were working together to rebuild the San Francisco water front.

D The fireworks that filled San Francisco during the Chinese New Year were dangerous and should be banned.

26 **What kind of work are the men shown in this photograph doing?**

F Bricklaying

G Cooking

H Sewing

J Teaching

27 **What would you guess a *sweatshop* was?**

A A crowded room where poorly paid workers worked long hours

B A large factory filled with up-to-date machinery

C A modern office where workers created and filed business records

D An underground room used for storage

28 **The men in the photograph were immigrants. What do you think drew them to the New World?**

F Better health care

G Cultural opportunities

H Jobs

J The climate

"Be a little careful, please!" he warned. "The hall is dark and you might stumble over the children pitching pennies back there. Not that it would hurt them; kicks and cuffs are their daily diet. They have little else. Here where the hall turns and dives into utter darkness is a step, and another, another. . . Here is a door. Listen! That short hacking cough, that tiny, helpless wail—what do they mean?—Oh! a sadly familiar story—before the day is at an end. The child is dying of measles. With half a chance it might have lived; but it had none. That dark bedroom killed it."

From an account written by Jacob Riis in 1890

We are sometimes asked in the name of patriotism to forget the merits of this fearful conflict and to remember with equal admiration those who struck at the nation's life and those who struck to save it—those who fought for slavery and those who fought against it. I am no minister of malice: I would [not] strike the fallen foe. I would [not] repel the repentant, but may my right hand forget her cunning and my tongue cleave to the roof [of] my mouth if I forget...the difference between the respective parties to that protracted, bloody, and terrible conflict.

From a speech given by Frederick Douglass at Arlington National Cemetery in 1871

29 **This passage is mainly about —**

A   children's games

B   inner city housing

C   poverty and disease

D   tolerance and intolerance

30 **What is the author's attitude towards the situation he describes?**

F   He is bitterly angry that people live in such terrible conditions.

G   He is desperately worried about catching the measles himself.

H   He is hopeful that reforms will improve human lives.

J   He is pleased that the children know how to amuse themselves.

31 **This passage comes from a book Riis wrote telling middle-class Americans about life in cities. What do you think he called his book?**

A   *How the Other Half Lives*

B   *Job Opportunities for Immigrants*

C   *Public Health and Public Services*

D   *The American Dream*

32 **Frederick Douglass hoped to persuade his listeners that —**

F   both sides had good reasons for fighting the other

G   no one should ever forget how many lives were lost in the Civil War

H   the bitterness caused by the Civil War should finally be forgotten

J   they should never forget that the war was fought between those who supported slavery and those opposed to it.

33 **What does Douglass mean when he says, "I am no minister of malice"?**

A   He believes in forgiving those who regret their misdeeds.

B   He believes in good as well as evil.

C   He believes some people are born bad.

D   He used to be a Southern Baptist.

34 **You might infer from Douglass's speech that he spent most of his life —**

F   fighting racial oppression and injustice

G   teaching students about patriotism

H   trying to understand God's word

J   writing about the Civil War

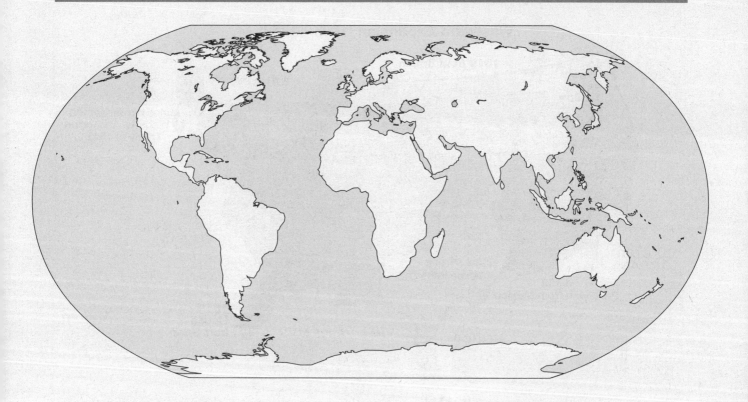

35 Label the four oceans and the seven continents on this map of the world.

36 Identify the projection used by this map and explain its advantages over the Mercator projection.

_____

_____

_____

_____

_____

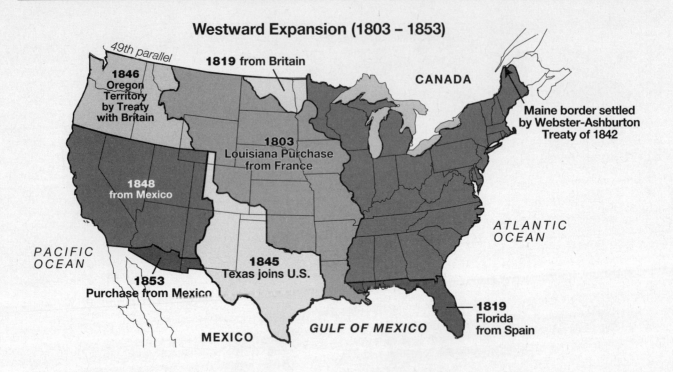

Westward Expansion (1803 – 1853)

49th parallel

1846 Oregon Territory by Treaty with Britain

1819 from Britain

CANADA

Maine border settled by Webster-Ashburton Treaty of 1842

1803 Louisiana Purchase from France

1848 from Mexico

ATLANTIC OCEAN

PACIFIC OCEAN

1853 Purchase from Mexico

1845 Texas joins U.S.

1819 Florida from Spain

MEXICO

GULF OF MEXICO

37 Complete the empty time line below using the events shown on the map. Give the time line a title.

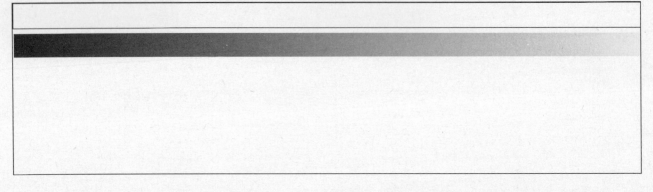

38 If the time line were expanded to 1763, which of these events should be included?

F The arrival in the Americas of people from Siberia 18,000 years ago

G The conquest of Mexico by Hernan Cortés

H The Peace of Paris by which Britain won the French lands east of the Mississippi

J The terms of the peace that ended the Civil War

39 Which of the following did *not* help to settle the boundary between the United States and Canada?

A The British-American Convention of 1818-1819 regarding lands north of Louisiana Territory

B The Gadsden Purchase from Mexico of 1853

C The Oregon Cession

D The Webster-Ashburton Treaty

In South Asia, tea is grown on the southern slopes of the Himalayas. Farmers grow cotton and sugar-cane on the Indus-Ganges Plain. Cotton is grown on the Deccan plateau and woven into textiles in local factories. The Deccan is rich in minerals such as iron and limestone that are used in India's large steel industry.

Rice is the main crop of Southeast Asia and southern China. China also grows sugar cane and tea in the south and wheat, cotton, and silk in the north. Indonesia's large plantations produce sugar cane and rubber. China has a giant's share of the region's fuel deposits. It has large reserves of coal and some offshore oil. Indonesia also contains major oil and gas deposits. Beneath China's soil lie quantities of iron ore (which are made into steel) and other important minerals. China remains a largely agricultural nation, but it has built up its industries in recent years and is now a major exporter of manufactured goods.

Resource-poor Japan must import fuel or produce hydroelectric power from its swift-flowing rivers. Even so, it is the region's leading industrial power and produces steel, cars, electronic goods, and computer chips. Many of the other nations that rim the Pacific, particularly Hong Kong, South Korea, and Taiwan, have also developed their industries and become major exporters of consumer goods.

This passage identifies major crops, minerals, and industries found in South, Southeast, and East Asia.

40   Identify on the map where in Asia the crops named in the passage are grown.

41   Identify on the map where in Asia the mineral resources named in the passage are to be found.

42   Identify on the map where in Asia the industries identified in the passage are located.

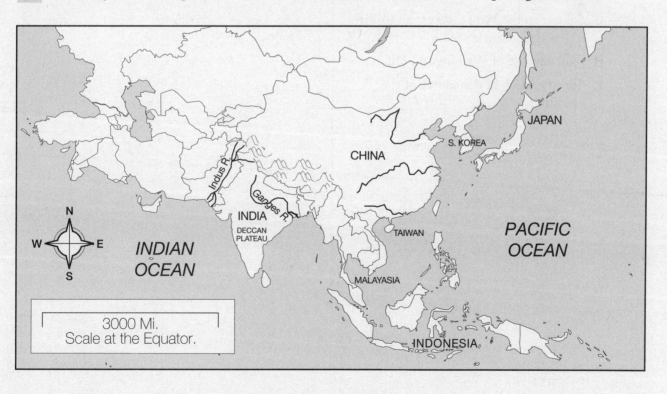

> To Oliver Ames, North Easton, *[President of the Union Pacific Railroad Board]*
>
> The last rail was laid today connecting the Union Pacific with the Central Pacific at Promontory. This act quietly performed 2500 miles west of Boston, 690 miles east of Sacramento, will have an influence upon the future and upon the commerce and travel of the world that no one can today estimate. We congratulate you upon the success of the enterprise.
>
> *John Duff, Sidney Dillon, Thomas Durant, G.M. Dodge, 1869*

43 This letter refers to —

   A a secret and illegal business enterprise

   B the completion of the rail link between the United States' east and west coasts

   C the first railroad built in the United States

   D the future of commerce in the U.S.

44 Bearing in mind that the U.S. is about 3,000 miles wide and Boston is on the east coast, you can conclude that Promontory was —

   F closer to the East Coast than to the West Coast

   G closer to the West Coast than to the East Coast

   H just outside of Washington, D.C.

   J pretty much in the center of the nation

45 Which of the following do you think was the most likely consequence of the event described in the letter?

   A Canals were built alongside the tracks.

   B Sacramento became the state capital of California.

   C The Union Pacific Railroad became bankrupt.

   D Villages and towns near the railroad tracks began to prosper.

An immigrant family gazes at the Statue of Liberty

46 **What message is contained in this photograph?**

F An immigrant family honors a symbol of the freedom they hope to find in the United States.

G Immigrants needed jobs to allow them to feed their families.

H Most immigrant families were small.

J New York City was filled with sights and monuments that amazed immigrants fresh from the farms of the Old Country.

47 **What might be a consequence for families like the one shown above of the event described in the letter on p. 188?**

A They would be able to travel by train to California and settle there.

B They would find work building the railroad.

C They would have luxury items shipped to them in New York from Sacramento.

D They would pay a tourist visit to Promontory.

In 1803 President Jefferson ordered his secretary Meriwether Lewis and Capt. William Clark to lead an expedition to explore the lands of Louisiana Territory, which he had purchased from France. Portions of the letter, below, tell Lewis what he should look out for. The maps on the next page were drawn shortly after the expedition.

To Meriwether Lewis, esquire, captain of the first regiment of infantry of the United States of America:

. . . The object of your mission is to explore the Missouri River, and such principal streams of it, as, by its course and communication with the waters of the Pacific Ocean, whether the Columbia, Oregon, Colorado, or any other river, may offer the most direct and practicable water-communication across the continent, for the purposes of commerce.

Beginning at the mouth of the Missouri, you will take observations of latitude and longitude, at all remarkable points on the river, and especially at the mouths of rivers, at rapids, at islands, and other places and objects distinguished by such natural marks and characters, of a durable kind, as that they may with certainty be recognized hereafter . . . The interesting points of the portage [carrying boats and supplies overland between two rivers] between the heads of the Missouri, and of the water offering the best communication with the Pacific ocean, should also be fixed by observation...

Although your route will be along the channel of the Missouri, yet you will endeavour to inform yourself, by inquiry, of the character and extent of the country watered by its branches, and especially on its southern side. The North river, or Rio Bravo, which runs into the gulf of Mexico, and the North river, or Rio Colorado, which runs into the gulf of California, are understood to be the principal streams heading opposite to the waters of the Missouri, and running southwardly. Whether the dividing grounds between the Missouri and them are mountains or flat lands, what are their distance from the Missouri, the character of the intermediate country, and the people inhabiting it, are worthy of particular inquiry. The northern waters of the Missouri are less to be inquired after, because they have been ascertained to a considerable degree....

Thomas Jefferson, President of the United States of America

48 Part of the route taken by Lewis and Clark is shown on the map at the top of the next page. It is a grey line running alongside the Missouri River. Draw in the route on the unlabeled map at the bottom of the next page. Based on President Jefferson's instructions, label the other two rivers he mentions in his last paragraph.

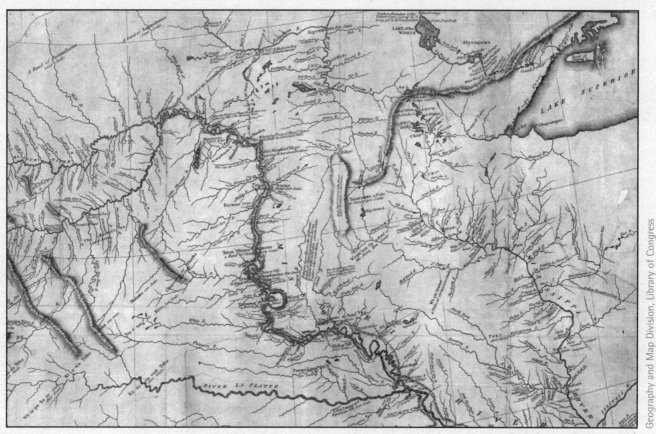

1814 Map of the first part of Lewis and Clark's route along the Missouri River.

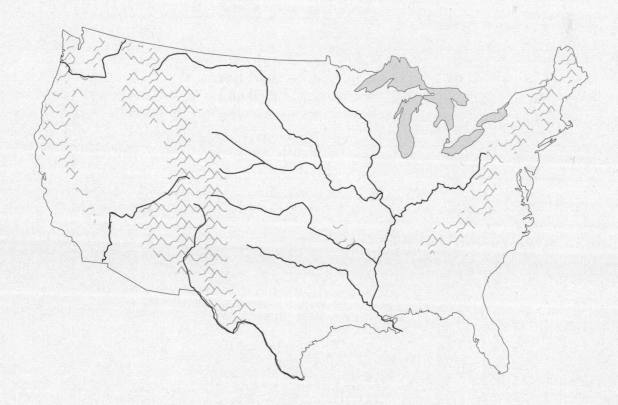

49   Lewis and Clark did finally reach the Pacific Ocean. How did they and their boats probably travel after arriving at the headwaters of the Missouri River?

_____

_____

_____

_____

_____

_____

_____

_____

_____

50   Using information from the maps on the previous pages, answer President Jefferson's
questions regarding the territory along Lewis and Clark's route.

_____

_____

_____

_____

_____

_____

_____

_____

_____